THE BREWPUB EXPLORER

of the
Pacific Northwest

THE BREWPUB EXPLORER OF THE PACIFIC NORTHWEST

Hudson Dodd
Matthew Latterell
Lani MacCormack
Ina Zucker

JOHNSTON
ASSOCIATES
INTERNATIONAL

P. O. BOX 313
MEDINA, WASHINGTON 98039
(206) 454-3490 ▪ FAX: (206) 462-1335
ONLINE ADDRESS: jasibooks@aol.com

The Brewpub Explorer *of the Pacific Northwest*, First Edition.
@ Copyright1996 by Hudson Dodd, Mathew Latterell, Lani MacCormack and
Ina Zucker

ISBN 1-881409-16-3

Book design by Mike Jaynes, Commercial Design & Illustration

Graphics images courtesy of Hudson Dodd, Mathew Latterell, Lani MacCormack
and Ina Zucker

Disclaimer
Although diligent efforts have been made to confirm the accuracy of information contained in this work, neither the publisher nor the author is responsible
for errors or inaccuracies or for changes occurring after publication. This work
was not prepared under the sponsorship, license, or authorization of any business, attraction, or organization described, depicted, or discussed herein.

JASI
Post Office Box 313
Medina, Washington 98039
(206) 454-3490 FAX: (206) 462-1335
Online Address: jasibooks@aol.com

Printed in the United States of America

Library of Congress cataloging-in-Publication Data

The brewpub explorer of the Pacific Northwest/Hudson Dodd...[et al.].
    — 1st ed.
        p.   cm.
    Includes index.
    ISBN 1-881409-16-3
    1. Bars (Drinking establishments)—Northwest, Pacific—Guidebooks.
2. Microbreweries—Northwest, Pacific—Guidebooks. 3. Beer.
I. Dodd, Hudson, 1967-
TX950.57.N8B73 1996
647.95795—dc20
                                        96-26576
                                        CIP

Table of Contents

Acknowledgment 1

Introduction 3
    Craft Brewing Terminology...4
    Beer Styles..5
    The Brewing Process 7
    Contract Brewing..8
    Travel Tips 9
    Helpful Phone Numbers..9

Touring the Pacific Northwest Brews:
Convenience Store Style 10

Oregon..13
    Listings 15
    Coming Attractions..65

Washington 73
    Listings 75
    Coming Attractions..130

British Columbia 135
    Listings 137
    Coming Attractions..163

Appendices
    Glossary of Brewing Terms..165
    You-Brew/Brew-On-Premise Facilities 177
    Home Brewing Suppliers 181

Index..185

Maps

Oregon 12

Eugene 24

Portland Metro...41

Washington 72

Seattle...88

British Columbia 134

Vancouver 141

Special Features

The Eugene Brewpub Scene 25

Portland – Beervana of the Northwest..................39

McMenamins Pubs & Breweries – A Neighborhood Place for Family & Friends...66

The Seattle Alehouse Experience.........................89

Washington's "Fourth Corner:...........................103

Virtual Tours 132

Vancouver, British Columbia 139

The Okanagan Valley Brew Tour 155

Acknowledgement

The authors would like to express their thanks to:

*Our families and friends
for their support, advice and encouragement;*

*The brewers, brewpub owners and managers
for their time and generosity;*

*And especially to Harry Bondareff, Chuck Dingee,
Todd Ebersole and Isabel Wyss, Doug Ferguson,
Ibrahim Hamide, Christian Krogstad, Mary Kurlinski,
Ravi Myers, Steve Richter, Lisa and Rick Schessler,
Geoff Twyman and Paul Wasik.*

A revolution in brewing and beer drinking has been sweeping North America since the mid-1980s. The flavors, quality, and local charms of "microbrews" (ales and lagers produced in limited batches by small breweries) are re-educating our palates and redefining what we think of as "good beer." Nowhere is this more true than in the Pacific Northwest, the birthplace of the microbrewing revolution.

Prior to Prohibition, local breweries were common throughout the United States. Small-town breweries and brewpubs served ales and lagers to friends and neighbors, and workers would fill up buckets of beer on their way home in the evening. Prohibition shut down nearly all these operations by the early 1920s. The repeal of Prohibition a short time later produced a legacy of regional and national breweries that still exists in the U.S. and Canada today. The small, neighborhood breweries, seemingly, were gone forever.

In the late 1970s, however, local brewing got a much needed jump-start. Fritz Maytag took over the then-failing Anchor Steam Brewing Company of San Francisco (one of the few craft breweries to survive Prohibition) and began to expand its brewing operation and distribution. Its growth and success inspired others, especially in the Pacific Northwest, to bring local brewing back to the neighborhoods. In 1982, Redhook Ales of Seattle opened its doors in the Fremont neighborhood. Today, Redhook is one of the biggest microbreweries in North America. British Columbia's Horseshoe Bay Brewing also opened in 1982, reviving the traditions of local brewing in Canada's western-most province. Two years later, Bridgeport Brewing Company christened Oregon's first microbrewery in over 60 years, followed by the phenomenally successful McMenamins family of brewpubs and taverns.

The Pacific Northwest brewing culture is setting the standards for microbrews across the continent, with annual production of regional brewers increasing nearly 50% a year. This is supported by the wild enthusiasm of the highest per capita population of microbrew drinkers in North America.

The revival of local brewing in the Pacific Northwest has also produced a diversity of styles and brewing approaches that vary wildly within the region. Oregon State has the most breweries and brewpubs per capita anywhere outside Europe. Washington is home to two of the largest microbreweries in North America: Redhood Ales and Pyramid Brewery Inc. And while the brewers south of the border are primarily ale breweries, British Columbia has refined the art of lagering, reviving the smooth, rich flavors produced at the turn of the century.

It is this exciting and dynamic brewing culture that inspired the creation of this book. We offer it as a celebration of the outstanding ales and lagers produced throughout the region and of the brewers and breweries that produce them. Use it in that celebratory spirit as you start out on your educational, fun and flavorful tour of the microbreweries and brewpubs of the Pacific Northwest.

Craft Brewery Terminology - What's Covered in This Book

The overall content of this book covers craft breweries, as distinct from industrial breweries. Explained below are some terms and working definitions that you'll hear throughout the Pacific Northwest beer scene (see also Glossary, page 165).

"Craft brewery" is a catch-all term for any size brewery producing "hand-crafted" beers, a term that connotes attention to the finer points of brewing without compromising quality in the name of quantity – though several craft breweries are now producing large quantities of beer. What differentiates these beers from industrial beers is the attention to the brewing process and the more-or-less strict adherence to tradition in utilizing only the ingredients of malted barley, hops, yeast and water without adjuncts or pasteurization. Craft breweries may, for instance, make beers containing wheat or rye, but not rice or corn, adjuncts used by industrial breweries.

Within this overall field are the two subsets referred to throughout the book – microbreweries and brewpubs. The term "microbrewery" is most widely recognized by the general public and is used as a synonym for "craft brewery." Technically, a microbrewery is a craft brewery of limited size, commonly categorized by less than 20,000 barrels in annual production. However, we have included some of the larger craft breweries under this umbrella. A "cottage brewery" is even smaller than a microbrewery, commonly categorized by less than 10,000 barrels in annual production.

A "brewpub" is simply a public drinking establishment that serves beers brewed on the premises. Generally, these establishments also serve food in a restaurant atmosphere, as well as other beverages besides beer. The term "brewhouse" is technically the area where the actual mashing and brewing occurs and consists primarily of the mash tun, lauter tun and kettle. However, this term has also become synonomous with "brewpub."

Within these already blurry delineations, however, there are even grayer areas. For instance, brewpubs are theoretically establishments that sell their beer only on the premises. But some also distribute their product to restaurants or pubs. In other cases, a microbrewery might have a deluxe tasting room which, though not a brewpub (because the brewery concentrates on off-premise sales), has the feel of one and offers a limited menu. In other cases, the brewery strictly sells kegs wholesale, but happens to reside in the same building as a restaurant or pub which buys and serves the brewery's beers, lending it a brewpub-like feel.

Beer Styles - What's the Difference Between a Lager and an Ale?

The names of beer styles such as Pilsner, Stout, and Best Bitter originated in Europe centuries ago in regions which, to a great extent, remained remote from each other until the modern era. These isolated hamlets and valleys had their own wild yeast strains which caused the actual fermenting process, though early brewers were oblivious to yeast's existence. Varying supplies of grains, malting facilities and hop types led to diverse recipes for making beer. In this way, regions gave birth to different beer styles.

With increased trade in Europe, these original European styles evolved over time and blended together somewhat. When the beers were brought to the New World, traditional styles soon took on unique twists. This was partly due to the differences between indigenous grains and yeasts and partly because of the North American settlers' independent spirits. Many of the new American styles took hold and survive to this day, including such old favorites as Cream Ale and Mild Brown Ale. Though many European and American beer styles are distinctly different, this book offers basic working definitions for the most common styles (see Glossary, page 165) and reflect the most enduring traditional characteristics. However, ours is certainly not the final word. There are books attempting to explain the differences between English Brown Ales and American Brown Ales. While such discussions are interesting, this book does not delve into these controversies.

In the 19th century, when yeast was discovered as the actual cause of fermentation, brewing began evolving into the scientifically defined endeavor it is today. Along with this important discovery came the realization that there are myriad strains of yeast, each lending very different characteristics to the finished beer, each behaving differently during fermentation. The two main branches of yeast strains are ale yeasts and lager yeasts. Ale yeasts are the most common naturally-occuring strains, fermenting at room temperature and rising to the top of the brew on the carbon dioxide bubbles they create. Lager yeasts are rarer in nature, requiring colder fermentation temperatures and settling to the bottom of the brew.

The isolation of lager-strain yeasts created a revolution in brewing. By the turn of the 20th century, the lighter-bodied, crisper-tasting lagers had become the beer of choice over ales throughout much of the world. And the revolution just kept growing, along with the spread of the modern cooling equipment necessary for lager brewing. Though Britain was the last hold-out of devout ale drinkers, today, there is an ale renaissance throughout many parts of the world, most notably North America. Lager continues as the leading beer style internationally, however.

The Brewing Process -
What's in This Stuff Anyway?

The basics of brewing are just that – pretty basic. While this is not a book on how to brew, here's a brief description of the process.

Beer is made from fermented grain, with barley the grain of choice. Before the grain is fermented, it's turned into malt by means of a subtle and intricate process developed over centuries of experimentation. First the grain is soaked in water, then allowed to begin germination. Just as germination begins, the mix is whisked into a roasting oven called a kiln. Here the grain is roasted to varying degrees. The resulting product is malt.

Breweries purchase the malt, then crack the intact husks in a mill. The cracked malt or grist is poured either by hand or, more commonly, via an auger system into the mash tun. The grist is cooked or mashed in water in this large vessel. Temperature is held steady in order to extract the enzymes and proteins. The soupy mix is then pumped into the lauter tun where the spent grains are rinsed with hot water or "sparged" and removed from the liquid (called sweet wort). The sweet wort is pumped into a kettle and boiled. Hops are added at various times during the boil depending on what properties the brewer desires – aroma, bitterness, etc. Many kettles are equipped with a whirlpool mechanism, which collects the hops and undissolved proteins at the end of the boil and flushes them out of the finished wort. Some breweries employ separate whirlpools or other devices known as hop jacks to remove the sediments from the wort.

The wort is now ready to ferment (which happens when the yeast metabolizes the sugars and converts them into alcohol and carbon dioxide), but it's still much too hot from the long boil for yeast to survive. So it's cooled in a heat exchanger and sent to the fermentation tank. Then the yeast is pitched or added to the wort.

After a period of time determined by the strain of yeast and the recipe of the wort, but roughly equal to a week, the beer is transferred or "racked" to the conditioning tank, leaving the unwanted sediment behind. Here the yeast is allowed to finish metabolizing as high a percentage of sugars in the wort as possible, and the remaining sediment is allowed to settle out of the beer. The time a brew spends in a conditioning tank is also dependent on the kind of beer made – anywhere from a few days to several months. The conditioning tank is kept at room temperature for top-fermenting yeasts or chilled for bottom-fermenting yeasts.

The beer is now ready for consumption. It can be filtered at this time to achieve greater clarity than conditioning generally yields. The beer is racked into a bright tank from which beer can be served to a customer or held before bottling or kegging.

Contract Brewing - Why Isn't That Beer with The Green Label in Here?

Contract brewing is the perfectly logical result of a burgeoning demand for craft beer. With a seemingly ever-increasing market, there is ample opportunity for anyone who knows how to make a decent beer to sell it. The main hindrance to entering the nouveau beer marketplace is the capital required to build a brewery. Several brewing ventures have bypassed this obstacle by striking deals with industrial breweries to brew their recipes, and then market the beer as "micro-brewed." Similarly, all of the major industrial breweries have targeted microbrew drinkers with phantom craft brews often sporting local-sounding names as the brewery of origin.

Since this is a guidebook to microbreweries, it does not include information on contract beers. You won't find information on Emerald City Ales, Oregon Ales, Jet City Ales or Pete's Wicked Ales (all of which have brewing contracts in the Northwest), because they are beers without a brewery. Their absence is in no way a judgement on the merits of these products.

However, several of the breweries in this book have contracts to brew "house beers" for other establishments, commonly restaurants. This is a different phenomenon altogether, where the brewing establishment is its own brewery and just happens to brew special lines of beer for other venues.

Travel Tips

Travel safely – select a designated driver at the outset of any brewery tour! Remember, once you've started, it's too late. Drinking and driving is simply not an option, so if you're going to drive to the establishments listed in this book, make sure the person behind the wheel is not sampling brews along the way.

Helpful Phone Numbers for the Brew Tourer

For Road Conditions

BC Highway Patrol: 604/869-7760

Oregon Highway Patrol: 503/976-7277 or 541/889-3999

Washington Highway and
Mountain Pass Conditions: 900/407-7277

BC Ferries

Schedules change regularly. Call for current schedules
and reservation information.

BC Ferries
Marketing and Public Relations
1112 Fort Street
Victoria, BC V8V 4V2

Vancouver: 604/277-0277

Victoria: 604/386-3431

Nanaimo: 604/753-6626

BC Web URL: http://bcferries.bc.ca/ferries

Washington State Ferry System

Schedules change quarterly. Reservations are offered on the Anacortes, WA-Sidney, BC, route only and are accepted starting mid-May for travel mid-June through mid-September.

Washington State Ferry
Public Affairs Office
Colman Dock
801 Alaskan Way, Pier 52
Seattle, WA 98104

Seattle: 206/464-6400

WA State: 1/800/843-3779

TDD Callers: 1/800/833-6388

Telebraille Callers: 1/800/833-6385

Touring the Pacific Northwest Brews:
Convenience Store Style

Your local grocery store has just added a new line of beers to the standard line-up of domestic beers. The labels are eye-catching and proudly proclaim that these beers are microbrewed. Better yet, they are from the Pacific Northwest, the region leading the current microbrewery revolution. Curiosity, relief and exhilaration are common responses from customers. Finally, you can taste for yourself what everyone has been talking about. You grab a few delicious-sounding choices and head for home, triumphant. But is the beer you've selected really a microbrew?

As interest in quality, hand-crafted ales and lagers continues to grow, so does the number of brewers, styles, labels, trademarks, etc. How can you be sure the bottle you bought at the store is really a tasty Pacific Northwest brew? Enter the Oregon Brewers Guild and similar member organizations in Washington and British Columbia. These associations represent microbreweries and brewpubs throughout the Pacific Northwest and work to promote the tastes, quality, and brewing culture that have made this region famous.

The Oregon Brewers Guild, founded in 1992, has quickly become an important resource for brewers, beer enthusiasts and other brewing organizations throughout North America. Recently, the Guild confronted Oregon Ale, a marketing company distributing faux Oregon microbrews throughout the United States. Oregon Ale showed up on grocery shelves around the country. This should have been a great thing for regional brewers, except for one problem: There is no Oregon Ale and Beer brewery. Brewed under contract by other breweries, Oregon Ale, and similar "contract" brews may not necessarily reflect the representative styles and quality of the region they claim as home. The Oregon Brewers Guild is currently conducting a "truth in labeling" campaign to require brewers to disclose their company name or brewery location on bottle labels, so that the unique culture and flavors of truly microbrewed ales are properly identified.

Representing nearly all of Oregon's breweries, the Guild's logo identifies members' beers. Larger regional breweries, such as Full Sail in Hood River, are incorporating this logo to the designs of their six-pack holders, and brewpubs will often proudly display their Guild membership on table tents and coasters.

So how do you know if that "microbrew" you just picked up at the corner store is really from the Pacific Northwest? Look for the brewery name or location on the label. Or look for the Oregon Brewers Guild logo on the six-pack holder to make certain that the beer you are about to purchase is really from a Pacific Northwest microbrewery or brewpub.

For more information about the Oregon Brewers Guild and other brewery organizations in the Pacific Northwest and throughout North America contact:

Oregon Brewers Guild
510 NW 3rd Avenue
Portland, OR 97209
503/295-1862
Fax: 503/226-4895
Web URL: http://www.oregonbeer.org/~beer
E-mail address: beer@teleport.com

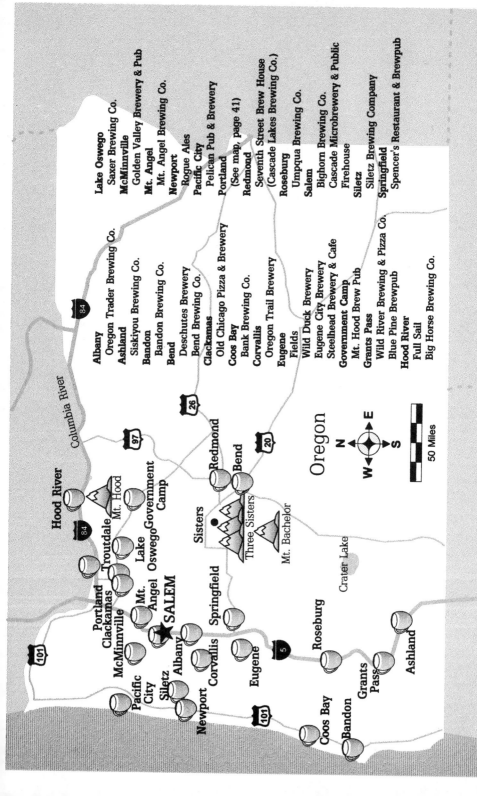

OREGON

Oregon is doubly blessed by its incredible beauty and its abundance of hand-crafted beers. With more breweries per capita than anywhere else outside Europe, the state is a leader in the microbrewing revolution, influencing styles, flavors and the brewing culture throughout North America.

No matter where you travel in Oregon – from the rugged coastline to the towering peaks of the Cascades, in the little towns scattered throughout the state or in Portland, brewing capitol of the continent, outstanding beer awaits.

Oregon is also home to the McMenamins empire, one of the essential forces in jump-starting the current microbrewing renaissance. McMenamins, which operates taverns and brewpubs throughout Oregon and Washington, is joined by more than 40 other breweries in producing some of the finest ales and lagers available anywhere in North America.

Bandon Brewing Company

P.O. Box 1270
Bandon, OR 97411
541/347-4827

Established: 1993

Hours: Call for tours

Children: Yes

Food: No

Entertainment: No

Smoking: No

Payment: No retail sales

Takeout: No

Directions: Bandon is on Highway 101 south of Coos Bay on the Oregon Coast. Call for tours at least one week in advance.

Bob Hawkins, owner of the Bandon Brewing Company, describes his business as "every homebrewer's dream." This seven-barrel brewing system located next to Hawkins' house in the cranberry bogs of the southern Oregon Coast is the only Oregon brewery located at the brewer's home. While Bob does not offer public tours, he does conduct popular "hands-on" private tours on a limited basis, allowing visitors to participate in the brewing process.

Hawkins distributes his ales to several establishments in Bandon as well as along the southern Oregon Coast and further inland. Visitors interested in finding the brewery's "BogWater" Ales should check out Lloyd's, a true, small-town tavern. For a more upscale setting, head to House of Stewart just south of Bandon on Highway 101, or stay in town and enjoy the view of the Bandon riverfront and lighthouse from the Crows Nest atop the Wheelhouse Restaurant.

The Bandon Brewing Company currently produces four standard ales and a winter seasonal. The BogWater Wheat Ale is a medium bodied, lightly hoppy wheat ale. The BogWater Porter, a creamy darker ale neither too roasted nor too chocolately, is a favorite among the locals. BogWater Scotch Ale, now brewed as a standard by popular demand, is a sweet, malty, traditional-styled Scotch Ale with a high alcohol content to keep away the chills of winter. The company also produces a bitter, a spiced Winter Warmer and is working to produce a cranberry ale using fruit from the family's own cranberry fields.

Bank Brewing Company
201 Central
Coos Bay, OR 97420
541/267-0963

The Bank Brewing Company is a perfect combination of old and new. The 1924 building was once a bank. Today, copper brew kettles stand where the bank manager worked and the serving tanks are safely protected in the vault. A full restaurant menu highlighting gourmet pizzas and weekend specials, including a "catch of the day," is sure to satisfy the hunger of both regular customers and the wind-blown visitor.

The brewery offers six standard ales and several seasonals. Crowd favorite Bull Buck Bitter, a wonderfully hoppy amber ale, is a well-crafted version of a traditional English Best Bitter. Tioga Black, brewed in the style of a Bavarian Schwarzbier (literally black beer), is a dark amber-colored beer with a malty, slightly roasted flavor – an outstanding beer rarely brewed in the Pacific Northwest. Bankers Stout, the darkest offering, is a rich, creamy, chocolate stout and will easily satisfy the tastes of stout enthusiasts. Seasonal Hallows Ale, a high alcohol Belgian-style ale, is an amber-colored sipping ale with a fruity finish and just a hint of coriander.

This is the first brewery in Coos Bay since the close of the Eagle Brewing Company in 1912 and a welcome addition to Oregon's south coast. The town is just minutes from the coast and is a perfect base for exploring the Oregon Dunes National Recreation Area or the cliffs and beaches around Charleston.

Established: 1995

Hours: 11:30 am-10 pm Monday-Thursday, 11:30 am-midnight Friday and Saturday

Children: Yes

Food: Excellent pizzas, full menu

Entertainment: Darts, televised sporting events, occasional live jazz or blues

Smoking: Yes, in bar area

Payment: Visa/MC

Takeout: Yes

Directions: From Highway 101 going south: Turn right on Central Avenue in downtown Coos Bay. Brewery is visible on left after one block. From Highway 101 going north: Turn left on Commercial. Turn left on Highway 101. Turn right on Central Avenue and go one block.

Rogue Ales Bay Front Public House

748 SW Bay Boulevard
Newport, OR 97365
541/265-3188

The Bay Front Public House was originally Rogue's second pub, opening six months after Ashland's Rogue Brewery & Public House (now Siskiyou Brewing). Today, the pub is an integral part of the bustling Newport waterfront tourist heaven, though it serves more locals than tourists.

Inside, the brewpub is sparsely lit and features wooden paneling and brass rails. Rogue beer memorabilia lines the walls. The main room with its large square bar is the smoking area, with an additional side room for non-smokers. The area of the building which originally housed the brewery now serves as a game room with pool tables, dart lanes and Oregon lottery machines.

The menu is extensive with the usual burgers and beer-battered fish & chips, but also features entrees like *cioppino* (seafood stew), baked red snapper and some appealing pasta dishes. The bar has 22 beer handles, pouring the complete line of Rogue Ales, along with a few guest taps. Local favorites include the old standard American Amber Ale, the never-bottled Honey Cream Ale, and the thick, hoppy McRogue Scotch Ale.

After a pint or two, ask the bartender for a bathroom tour. The ceilings of two rooms, labeled only "hops" and "barley" for the discerning beer drinker, are both decorated with fluorescent renditions of the night sky. See if you can spot Venus. If not, you might need another taste of that McRogue.

Established: 1989

Hours: 11 am-11 pm or later daily

Children: Yes, with a special play area

Food: Full menu featuring pub fare, pasta, seafood

Entertainment: Winter: Fridays and Saturdays – live trivia show; Summer: occassional live music; television, pool, darts, lottery machines

Smoking: Yes, in separate areas

Payment: Visa/MC, Discover

Takeout: Yes

Directions: From Highway 101, turn east toward Newport's Old Town and Bay Front. Go all the way down the hill to Bay Blvd. and turn right. The public house is at the far end of the street on the right.

House of Rogues & Headquarters for the Intl. Assoc. of Rogues
3220 OSU Drive
Newport, OR 97365
541/867-3663

Established: 1992/1995

Hours: Summer: 11 am-6:30pm Monday-Sunday; Winter: 11 am-6:30pm Monday-Friday

Children: Yes at House of Rogues; No at Tasting Room

Food: Snacks

Entertainment: No

Smoking: Yes at House of Rogues, No at Tasting Room

Payment: Visa/MC, Discover

Takeout: Yes

The main Rogue brewery is located in an enormous, old marina building on the water. The 30-barrel brewhouse and extensive kegging and bottling operations occupy the better part of the building. Brewery tours are given regularly during the day. While you wait, you can sample Rogue brews on tap and sit at one of the picnic tables looking out over Newport Bay.

John "More Hops" Maier, brewer, has been brewing Rogue ales here since day one and is now a legend in Northwest microbrewing culture. His ales travel well for great distances, and Rogue president Jack Joyce credits Maier's heavy hand with both hops and malts for this trait, calling them virtually bullet-proof. Rogue's ales are now available in 35 states and three provinces both on draft and in bottles.

The House of Rogues, located less than a ½ mile from the brewery, is a combination tasting room and retail shop. Taking delight in the mischievous connotations of its name, the company has established the Rogues Gallery, where a photo and paraphenalia collection of "roguish" items is on display. And, of course, there are several Rogue Ales on tap for visitors.

Maier's beers have garnered great recognition. His Amber and Golden have both become standards for their respective styles. He also brews some of Oregon's most exotic brews, including Rogue Smoke, a Rauchbier with an intense hop finish; St. Rogue Red, roasty and piney, and Old Crustacean, a powerful barley wine that's malty, bitter, sweet and fruity all in one mouthful.

Directions: To House of Rogues: From Highway 101, turn east at the stoplight south of the Newport Bridge. Drive one block to the T and the House of Rogues is right in front of you.

Rogue Ales Brewery & South Beach Tasting Room
3135 SE Ferry Slip Rd.
South Beach, OR 97366
541/867-4131

To Brewery/Tasting Room: From Highway 101 northbound, turn east at the stoplight south of the Newport Bridge. At the T, turn north and drive ½ mile past the Newport Aquarium to the edge of the bay and turn west. The brewery is on your right. From Highway 101 southbound, take the first exit after the Newport Bridge. It curves under the bridge headed east. The brewery is on your left.

Siletz Brewing Company
267 Gaither Street
Siletz OR 97380
541/444-7256

Established: 1995

Hours: 11 am-closing, daily

Children: Yes

Food: Full menu including pizza

Entertainment: Pool, darts, video poker, regularly televised sports, live music

Smoking: Yes

Payment: Visa/MC

Takeout: Yes

Directions: From Highway 101 in Newport, take Highway 20 to Corvallis. At the Dairy Queen, take 229 to Siletz. Brewpub is at the far end of town on left.

Located just a few miles inland from the Oregon Coast, the Siletz Brewing Company is the dream of partners Bud Shoemake, a former harbormaster for the Port of Newport, and Tony Dilley, who once worked in the regional fishing industry. Both now live alongside the Siletz River and are hard at work in their new brewery. The river plays an important role for the brewery: The ales are made from the mountain waters that lead into the Siletz.

The interior of the brewpub is sparsely decorated, with a few pictures covering the wood paneling on the walls. Video poker machines occupy one room, and the bar and a few tables take up the rest of the building. Currently, the brewery produces four standard ales. The Siletz SOS Pale Ale, a tasty and smooth malty ale with a crisp finish, is the pub favorite. The dry-hopped Amber will please anyone searching for an aromatic, richly hopped ale. A Nutbrown and a Porter round out the Siletz Brewing Company's fine line of ales.

Don't rush away from Siletz too quickly. Take a tour of the Community Center. Plan a visit in July, when the town hosts one of the biggest Pow-Wows in the region, then spend time kayaking or fishing on the Siletz. For a scenic drive, follow the river north until it empties into Siletz Bay on the Oregon Coast. The longer you stay in the area, the more you appreciate the beauty of the water and the mountains, and the more you enjoy the people who call this place home.

Siskiyou Brewing Company
31-B Water Street
Ashland, OR 97520
541/488-5061

Siskiyou Brewing Company is the new name for Ashland's former Rogue Brewery & Public House. In operation since 1988, the pub's long-time manager Patrick Couchman recently negotiated the change in ownership. The new identity and brews have been well received by locals and fit well with Southern Oregon's fiercely independent attitude.

The brewery produces five outstanding ales for local consumption, distribution and bottle sales. Jefferson Gold, a light golden ale with a clean, crisp finish, is the only Siskiyou brew currently available in bottles. Ashland Amber, a long-time offering of the brewery, is a malty ale with a well-balanced, hoppy flavor. Pilot Rock Porter, Siskiyou Pale and Jibber Ale, a richly malty Strong Ale, round out the brewery's offerings. If the weather is appropriate, relax with your Siskiyou brew out on the backdeck while enjoying one of the pub's delicious pizzas.

Ashland is a wonderful place. Nestled under Mt. Ashland, the town is home to Oregon's Shakespeare Festival. Ashland has a remarkable diversity of outstanding restaurants which flourish during the theater season from early spring to late fall. The Siskiyou Brewing Company pub is located next to Ashland Creek, and patrons sitting out on the expansive decks behind the pub can watch for salmon returning to the creek to spawn.

Established: 1988/1996

Hours: Winter: 4 pm-closing, daily. Summer: 11:30 am-closing, daily

Children: Yes

Food: Pizzas, pub fare

Entertainment: Darts, live music Saturday nights, board games

Smoking: No

Payment: Checks, Visa/MC

Takeout: Yes

Directions: From I-5, take exit 19. At the end of the off-ramp, turn left onto Highway 99. Take the first right past the second light onto Water Street

Blue Pine Brewpub

422 SW 5th Street #B
Grants Pass, OR 97526
541/476-0760

The Blue Pine Brewpub is easy to miss. This best-kept secret of Grants Pass is hidden between the historic Schmidt House and a hair salon. A small sign between two buildings is your only clue to finding the pub. Parking and access are easy from the rear of the establishment, which is housed in what was once the Grange Hall.

With its rough-cut, blue pine tables and bar made by the two owners, walls decorated in tie-dyed sheets, Grateful Dead and Jimi Hendrix posters, and a continuous open-mike music policy, the Blue Pine may astonish the unsuspecting visitor into feeling like they stepped back into the 60s. It has become home to a loyal clientele, who will stop by to have a drink, hang out and relax.

Five regular ales and several seasonals are brewed here. Rip Roarin' Red, the most popular, is a medium-colored ale with a slightly roasted flavor. Pearsoll Peak Pale, a light amber-colored ale, is milder and smoother, with little bitterness. Big Barley Brown, Blue Pine Porter and Midnite Stout, all progressively darker ales, are the brewery's three other regular offerings. Pumpkin Pie Spice, flavored with cinnamon and other spices, Christmas Red Spice Ale and Autumn Amber are a few of the seasonals you might find during the year.

One of Oregon's smallest breweries, the Blue Pine Brewpub was founded with the goal of brewing beer for and with friends. Its neighborly atmosphere, affordable food and quality beers can easily turn a quick visit into a lazy, relaxing afternoon or the perfect evening.

Established: 1993

Hours: 2 pm-11 pm
Tuesday-Saturday

Children: Yes

Food: Sandwiches, salads, soups

Entertainment Live music, board games, foosball

Smoking: No

Payment: Checks

Takeout: Yes

Directions: Take exit 55 off of I-5. Brewery is on 5th Street between I and J streets, between Governor's Mansion Hair Salon and Ace Bookkeepers.

Wild River Brewing & Pizza Company

249 North Redwood Hwy
Cave Junction, OR 97523
541/592-3556

595 NE "E" St.
Grants Pass, OR
97526
541/471-7487

Wild River Brewing & Pizza Company had its beginnings as a 1970s pizza parlor in Cave Junction, Oregon. In 1990, the owners added a brewery to the establishment and hired Hubert Smith, an award-winning home brewer, to head the brewery. In 1994, the company expanded its total brewing capacity to 30,000 barrels a year, opening a 200-seat restaurant and brewery in Grants Pass.

The Wild River restaurant in Grants Pass is hard to miss. Tall ceilings, two levels of seating and a speed-boat greet the visitor in this beer connoisseur's paradise. The brewery, fully visible from every seat in the restaurant, produces five standard and five seasonal ales. Smith is a historical brewer, uncovering recipes from brewers' journals dating back to the 1700s and 1800s, and trying to recreate them with Pacific Northwest ingredients. His success is evident in his medal-winning Nutbrown Ale and Snug Harbor Old Ale. The Wild River Blackberry Porter is based on a 1750 Whitbread London porter, with blackberries added, and is easily one of the finest porters anywhere. The crowd favorite is an authentic German Hefeweizen, very different from the Northwest-style Hefeweizen made popular by Widmer Brewing and others.

The company also integrates beer into its food. All breads and pizza dough are made with spent grains produced in the brewing process, and many items in the extensive menu are flavored with Wild River brews. The authenticity and quality of the ales, coupled the pizzas and calzones cooked in the large wood-fired ovens, make Wild River a place you'll want to visit again and again.

Established: 1990

Hours: Monday-Friday, 7 am-10:30 pm, Saturday and Sunday 9 am-10:30 pm

Children: Yes

Food: Complete menu including breakfasts. Wood-fired pizzas and calzones are the specialties of the house

Entertainment: None

Smoking: No

Payment: Visa/MC

Takeout: Yes

Directions: Exit 55 off of I-5. Head west one mile. Wild River is at the corner of "E" and Mill Street.

Umpqua Brewing Company
328 SE Jackson Street
Roseburg, OR 97470
503/672-0452

Roseburg's only brewpub is a wonderful mix of old-world style and local charm. A dark wooden bar inside the long brick and wood building frames the collection of beer steins and bottles along the walls, creating the feeling of a small-town English pub.

Umpqua Brewing is also home to the best entertainment in town, with local and regional musicians playing jazz, blues, folk, rock and even reggae every Friday and Saturday night. And don't be surprised if you happen to hear a reading from one of Roseburg's budding poets.

The brewery produces more than 10 different beers at all times, offering something for everyone. Summer Wheat, a light, flavorful ale, is the crowd favorite. Roseburg Red, a medium-colored ale, is full of caramel and roasted flavors, with a wonderful fruity finish. Imperial Stout and No Doubt Stout, both with rich chocolate and roasted flavors, offer slight variations on traditional styles and should please stout enthusiasts. Perry's Old Ale, a rich, malty English-style ale with plenty of hops in the finish, and Double Red barley wine are both "must-try" seasonals.

The brewpub's logos are modeled after glyphs found on rocks in the region. The company chose these images because they reflect the history and culture of the Umpqua Valley, and the brewers were committed to producing ales as marvelous and enduring as the pictures. This commitment is evident in the beauty of the building, the variety of entertainment and the diversity of quality ales produced.

Established: 1991

Hours: 5 pm-closing Tuesday -Saturday, 5 pm-8 pm Sunday

Children: Yes, until 9 pm

Food: Gourmet pizzas, burgers, nachos

Entertainment: Live music every weekend, poetry readings, games, regularly televised sports

Smoking: No

Payment: Checks

Takeout: Yes

Directions: From I-5, take Exit 124. East onto Harvard, cross the Oak Street Bridge to the second light. Left on Stephens. Go two lights and turn right onto Diamond Lake. Go one block and turn right onto Jackson Street. Umpqua Brewing is 1½ blocks up Jackson on the right.

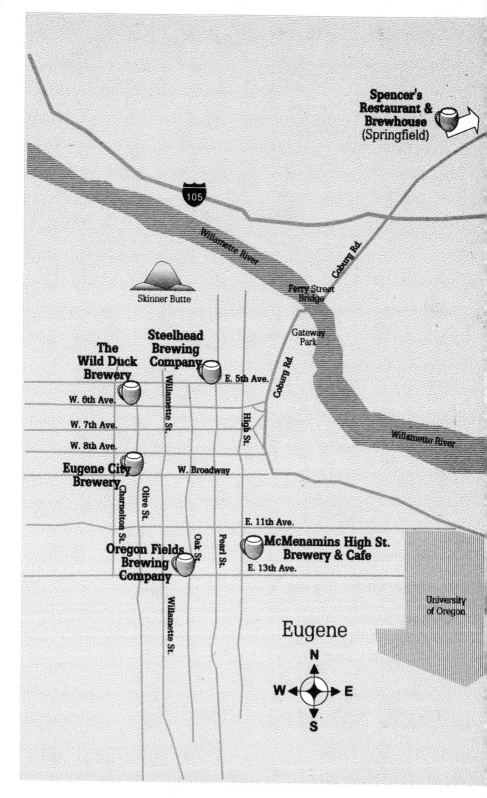

Spencer's Restaurant & Brewhouse (Springfield)

I-105

Willamette River

Coburg Rd.

Skinner Butte

Ferry Street Bridge

Gateway Park

Coburg Rd.

Steelhead Brewing Company

The Wild Duck Brewery

E. 5th Ave.

W. 6th Ave.

Willamette St.

W. 7th Ave.

High St.

W. 8th Ave.

Willamette River

Eugene City Brewery

W. Broadway

Chambelton St.

Olive St.

E. 11th Ave.

Oregon Fields Brewing Company

Oak St.

Pearl St.

McMenamins High St. Brewery & Cafe

E. 13th Ave.

Willamette St.

University of Oregon

Eugene

N
W   E
S

Eugene is a blessed city. Nowhere else in the Pacific Northwest – or perhaps anywhere outside Germany – can you find five brewpubs all within a few minutes' walk of each other. Fortunately, due to the combination of a relatively young population, a large University community, strong interest in dining out and the love of great beer, all five breweries thrive.

It's easy to plan a walking tour of Eugene's brewing operations, although something of a challenge to complete! Begin at High Street, Eugene's oldest microbrewery. McMenamins opened the High Street Brewery & Cafe in 1988 in a funky house at, appropriately enough, 1243 High Street (see page 68). Brewer Steve Van Rossem, working out of an amazingly cramped brewery below the Cafe, produces the standard McMenamins ales, as well as several wonderful originals.

Next, move on to Oregon Fields at 1290 Oak Street. Eugene's fourth oldest brewpub is the domain of brewer David Sohigian. If you can't decide what to try, ask the "Mug Club" regulars around the bar, or just grab a pint of the Dairyman's Old Ale, one of the brewery's finest offerings.

A few blocks' walk through the downtown area brings you to the Eugene City Brewery at 844 Olive Street. Afternoons you can shoot some pool for free at Mona Lizza, one of the two restaurants above the brewery. Brewer Tim Barr's favorite brew is Orca Pale Ale, a good representation of the style.

After a brief rest, walk the two blocks to Eugene's newest brewpub, the Wild Duck, at 169 W. 6th Avenue. The establishment offers a restaurant, full bar and concert hall complete with room for dancing. Brewer Glen Falconer's specialty is hops – make sure to try Glen's Best Bitter.

Finally, take a deep breath and walk over to Steelhead at 199 E. 5th Avenue. Teri Fahrendorf is the head brewer of Eugene's second oldest brewery. The Bombay Bomber, a flavorful India Pale Ale, has near cult status among beer drinkers in this town.

With five brewpubs in a city of just over 120,000 (plus Spencer's, Springfield's first brewpub just across I-5), it would be easy to suspect fierce competition and healthy amounts of secrecy and suspicion among the brewers. In traditional Eugene style, however, nothing could be further from the truth. Brewers have been known to share their yeast from time to time or borrow a particular hop or grain from each other. A recent and unique experiment, in which all the brewers took the same Brown Ale recipe and brewed it with their own yeast, equipment and unique styles, would be unthinkable almost anywhere else.

The Eugene brewing scene offers a wonderful collection of beers and styles served in relaxed, friendly establishments. Each pub and each brewer offers the visitor something refreshingly different. Collectively, they have created a remarkable celebration of beer and brewing.

Eugene City Brewery

844 Olive Street
Eugene, OR 97401
541/345-8489

The new Eugene City Brewery takes its name from Eugene's original brewery, which opened in 1866, just a few feet away from ECB's current location. Today, the brewery operates in the basement of two remarkable restaurants, West Brothers Bar-B-Que and Mona Lizza.

The restaurants, both owned by West brothers Mike, Jim and Phil offer an incredibly diverse menu. Open door number one and you enter West Brothers, specializing in barbecue and remarkably tasty and unique vegetarian entrees. Photos of barbecues from around the country adorn the walls above tables of hungry customers. Summers, outdoor seating is available under the mural of the original Eugene City Brewery building. Door number two reveals Mona Lizza, a smoke-free pasta and pizza restaurant offering six pool tables and darts. Mona Lizza is a beautiful place – bare brick work on the lower half of the walls, ornate mirrors above.

The brewery produces five standard ales and a rotating seasonal. Honey Orange Wheat, the crowd favorite, is a cloudy, honey-colored ale with a slightly citrus flavor. The Calcutta India Pale Ale is a fairly hoppy and somewhat bitter India Pale Ale with a mildly fruity finish. Black Hole Stout, creamy and chocolatey, has a devoted following among Eugene stout drinkers. Red Tape, a red-colored ale brewed with roasted barley and a smooth balance of malts and hops, is a unique ale definitely worth a try. Seasonals include a porter, barley wine, and brown.

Established: 1993

Hours: 11:30 am-11:30 pm daily

Children: Yes

Food: Two separate restaurants with extensive menus

Entertainment: Pool, darts, television

Smoking: No

Payment: Checks, Visa/MC, Am Ex, Diners Club

Takeout: Yes

Directions: From I-5 in Eugene, take the I-105 exit to the University of Oregon. Take I-105 until it ends at 7th. Turn left on 7th and go to Olive Street. Turn right on Olive. Brewery is on Olive between 8th and Broadway on the right side.

Oregon Fields Brewing Company

1290 Oak Street
Eugene, OR 97401
541/345-6584

The Oregon Fields Brewing Company has a little something for everyone. It's an upscale, art deco-styled restaurant with a creative and eclectic menu, and also a pub frequented by members of the "Mug Club," a group of over 200 regulars who come in and toss back pints from their very own mug. Fields is a terrific place for Sunday brunch with the whole family. And it is a quiet place to spend a rainy Eugene winter day, reading the paper and slowly finishing off a plate of nachos and a glass of beer.

Eight serving tanks standing above the bar in a long, glass-enclosed room divide the restaurant into two distinct areas. The front half, dominated by a beautiful oval bar, is home to the regulars. The back half contains two rows of cozy booths stretching toward the brewery, affording privacy and a place to indulge in quiet conversation.

Brewer David Sohigian has concocted four standard ales and five seasonals to date. Sohigian is particularly proud of the Organic Heferyzen, an unfiltered rye ale, similar to a Hefeweizen, and made almost entirely from organic grains (less than 1% is non-organic at present). Duck Tail, an amber-colored and very hoppy India Pale Ale, is named for the University's football team. Dairyman's Old Ale, a high alcohol, outstanding English Strong Ale, is the brewery's most popular offering. The Nomad Oatmeal Stout, a rich, velvety stout and a porter (occasionally flavored with marionberries) rotate as the brewery's darker selections.

Established: 1994

Hours: 11:30 am-midnight Monday-Saturday, 9 am-midnight Sunday

Children: Yes

Food: Extensive menu including Sunday brunch

Entertainment: Darts, regularly televised sporting events

Smoking: No

Payment: Checks, Visa/MC

Takeout: Yes

Directions: From I-5 in Eugene, take the I-105 exit to the University of Oregon. Take 105 to the Downtown exit. Cross over Ferry Street Bridge and take the exit for 8th Street and Downtown. Turn left on Pearl. Turn right on 11th, then left onto Willamette. Turn left on 13th. Brewery is at 13th and Oak on left side.

Steelhead Brewing Company

199 E. 5th Avenue
Eugene, OR 97401
541/686-2739

The Steelhead Brewing Company is Eugene's second oldest brewing operation. This busy and exciting pub is located in the middle of a thriving shopping and entertainment district on the edge of downtown Eugene, just a few blocks from the Hult Performance Center, the 5th Street Public Market and the beautiful Willamette River.

The inside of Steelhead is marvelous – cherry-stained mahogany tables and bar, an old "red box" English telephone booth, antique wood advertisements hanging on red brick walls and decadent wing-backed chairs you'll want to relax in for hours. For those not engrossed in conversation or drinking, several large televisions hang from the ceilings broadcasting the game.

The brewery has recently expanded, adding two new brewpubs in Burlingame and Irvine, California. Head Brewer Teri Fahrendorf has been shuttling between the three, getting the new pubs up to speed while working to keep up with demand at the Eugene operation. Steelhead brews three standard ales and a flurry of specials and seasonals. Always on tap are a Hefeweizen, a hoppy amber, and Bombay Bomber, a very fruity India Pale Ale with a strong hop finish. A variety of porters and stouts rotate as the brewery's dark ale, including Java Stout, brewed with roasted coffee beans to impart a strong coffee flavor. Other seasonals include a barley wine and a rye. The tasty Steelhead root beer is also always on tap and well worth a taste.

Established: 1991

Hours: 11:30 am-midnight Sunday-Thursday, 11:30 am-1 am Friday and Saturday

Children: No

Food: Upscale pub menu

Entertainment: Regular televised sporting events

Smoking: Half smoking

Payment: Checks, Visa/MC

Takeout: Yes

Directions: From I-5 in Eugene, take exit for I-105 to the University of Oregon. From I-105, take Downtown exit. Cross over Ferry Street Bridge and take the second right to 6th Street (99E). Turn right at bottom of ramp on High Street, go one block and turn left onto 5th. Go one block. Brewery is on right.

The Wild Duck Brewery

169 W. 6th Avenue
Eugene, OR 97401
541/485-3825

The Wild Duck, Eugene's newest brewpub, offers patrons and visitors a brewpub, restaurant and concert hall all under the same roof. The 500-person theater, with a completely modern sound system, promises to bring an eclectic mix of jazz, rock, reggae and more to the Eugene music scene. Combine this with quality ales brewed in-house, and the Wild Duck is sure to please.

The building is enormous, and except for the old gray concrete slab walls on its east face, it is impossible to guess that just last year this was a truck repair and rental shop. The bar and restaurant areas are remarkable – a gorgeous bar with two gold-inlaid German beer towers, huge and comical old-fashioned neon signs and a full view of the all-copper brewhouse. The Wild Duck also has an outside deck on the second floor – with a grill and bar.

Brewer Glen Falconer is passionate about beer. Stints at Rogue and Steelhead, and years of homebrewing, have only increased his love for brewing. The Wild Duck offers five standard ales and a rotation of seasonals. House favorite is the hoppy Duck Wheat Hefeweizen. Ringneck Stout is rich and chocolatey, and should attract many devoted stout fans. Glen's Best Bitter, Falconer's favorite brew, has an intense hop aroma and flavor. The beers of the Wild Duck all reveal Falconer's appreciation for hops, but none more than the seasonal Sasquatch Old Ale, a delightfully malty Strong Ale with a rich hoppy finish.

Established: 1996

Hours: 11:30 am-1 am Monday-Thursday, 11:30 am-2:30 am Friday and Saturday, 11:30 am-midnight Sunday

Children: Yes

Food: Upscale pub food

Entertainment: Live music, concerts

Smoking: Yes, in bar area

Payment: Checks, Visa/MC

Takeout: Yes

Directions: From I-5 in Eugene, take the University of Oregon exit to I-105. From I-105, take the Downtown exit. Cross over the Ferry Street Bridge and take the Downtown exit for 6th. Brewery is five blocks down 6th on the right.

Spencer's Restaurant & Brewhouse

980 Kruse Way
Springfield, OR 97477
541/726-1726

It took owner David Anderson more time than he would care to admit to open Springfield's first brewery. But if the restaurant mantra of "location, location, location" is true, Spencer's Restaurant & Brewhouse is doing most everything right. Located just off I-5 in the growing Gateway area of Springfield, Spencer's attracts tourists, business people and curious beer enthusiasts from Springfield's neighbor across I-5, Eugene.

The building was built specifically for Spencer's, with the brewery designed to head brewer Anders Johansen's specifications, and the rest of the establishment planned as a relaxed, family-style restaurant. The walls are covered with antique sports and gardening equipment, old mounted canned vegetable labels, and climbing ivy. A rich-grained oak bar is tucked back in the corner next to the fireplace. Spencer's is a restaurant dedicated to serving quality brews. Beer-battered fish and chips is the specialty of the house, and other seafood specials rotate nightly.

Spencer's offers four standards and a number of rotating seasonals. Mt. Baldy Extra Special Bitter, a fairly malty, higher alcohol ale with a crisp hoppy finish, is the brewer's favorite. Black Caddis Porter, decidedly thick and chocolately, is Spencer's darkest regular ale. Hofbrau Pilsner, a crisp and refreshing German lager, is one of the first lagers to be brewed in the local area and is delightful. Johansen designed the brewery to accommodate the long, cold conditioning required by lagers, and promises other styles to come.

Established: 1995

Hours:
11:30 am-11 pm daily

Children: Yes

Food: Pub menu with nightly specials including Ahi tuna and prime rib

Entertainment: TV at the bar

Smoking: No

Payment: Checks, Visa/MC, Am Ex

Takeout: Yes

Directions: From I-5, take exit 195 to Gateway/Springfield. At the first light turn right onto Kruse Way. Turn left at the first street (just past the IHOP). Brewery is on the left.

Oregon Trail

341 SW 2nd Street
Corvallis, OR 97333
541/758-3527

A visit to the Oregon Trail Brewing Company starts by stepping off 2nd Street in downtown Corvallis and into a beer garden that could have been transported straight from Bavaria. Located inside a three-story building, the beer garden was created with more than a little whimsy. The walls and ceilings are painted with clouds, blue sky, mountains, birds and small-town Bavarian scenes. The brewery, Old World Deli, and the home-brew store on the edges of the beer garden blend into this setting and look a little like Disney World's Main Street, complete with gingerbread-style storefront facades.

Ales are available on tap at the Old World Deli. Designed to take advantage of the building's three stories (the process starts on the top floor, moving downwards from kettle to fermenters to conditioners), the brewery has the distinction of being the only gravity-fed brewing system in the Oregon.

Oregon Trail brews six ales, including a very tasty Belgian-style White Ale complete with hops, coriander and orange-peel; an award-winning Brown Ale – a dry, hoppy, slightly roasted brown; a Kölsch-like Trail Ale, as well as a porter, stout and one seasonal. Recent seasonals have included a spiced Christmas Ale, the Morebock Bock and the strong-flavored End of the Trail Ale.

Established: 1987

Hours: 8 am-10 pm Monday-Saturday, 11 am-5 pm Sunday

Children: Yes

Food: Deli style sandwiches, soups

Entertainment: Live music on weekends

Smoking: No

Payment: Cash only

Takeout: No

Directions: From I-5, take exit 228 to Highway 34. Cross over the Willamette River and at 2nd turn left. Brewery is four blocks down on the left. Call in advance for tours.

Oregon Trader Brewing Company

140 Hill Street NE
Albany, OR 97321
541/928-1931

Established: 1993

Hours: 3 pm-8 pm Monday-Thursday, 12 pm-8 pm Friday and Saturday

Children: No

Food: Sandwiches, snacks

Entertainment: Darts, musicians about once a month

Smoking: No

Payment: Checks

Takeout: Yes

Directions: Take I-5 exit 234A or B to Main Street. Turn right to Water. Turn left on Hill Street NE.

A stop at the Oregon Trader Brewing Company serves two purposes: drinking beer and playing darts with friends. The brewery takes up one third of a large converted auto garage. Scattered tables fill the room, and customers like to debate the merits of various malts or hops, share homebrewing tall tales and chat with the owner about his latest brew.

Owner Jerry Mathern always wanted to find a way to brew beer for a living. In 1993, he opened the Oregon Trader, a small operation that somehow produces seven standard ales, always on tap, and a rotation of seasonals as well. The beer enthusiast will delight in the high-quality ales and lagers Mathern serves. Choose from a variety of offerings, from the rich, full-bodied chocolate and roasted flavors of the porter to the fairly explosive Green Chili Beer.

The crowd favorite at Oregon Trader is the Hefeweizen. Other standard offerings include Nutbrown, Scottish Ale, Oatmeal Stout and Amber Lager. Mathern brews a Berry Weizen, Belgian White, Bock, India Pale Ale and other beers on a seasonal rotation.

Albany is a town rich in the recent history of the Willamette Valley, with over 500 covered bridges and historic buildings. The pace of the city is just a bit slower than other large towns in the area. The quality beers and relaxed atmosphere of the Oregon Trader fit this area well.

Bighorn Brewing Company
515 12th Street SE
Salem, OR 97301
503/363-1976

Established: 1995

Hours: 11 am-2 am daily

Children: Yes

Food: Mix of Pub-and Tex-Mex-style foods

Entertainment: Regularly televised sporting events, pool, poker machines

Smoking: Yes, in separate areas

Payment: Checks, Visa/MC, Am Ex

Takeout: Yes

Directions: Take exit 253 off of I-5 in Salem. Head west into Salem on Mission Street. Take a right onto 13th just after crossing over the bridge. Brewpub is on the left at the first light.

The Bighorn Brewing Company is a recent addition to the Ram Border Cafe, a popular sports bar and restaurant in Salem. The building is enormous, with five separate seating areas and an outside patio overlooking Ditch Creek. The central area features a huge projection screen for viewing sporting events and a full bar. The 15-barrel brewing system, complete with four fermenters and five conditioners, is visible from three of the five rooms.

The Ram Border Cafe is one of a growing number of regional chains adding breweries to already successful restaurants. Hiring Tim Chamberlin, a 15-year veteran homebrewer, preserves much of the local character and regional flavor of the Bighorn brews.

Currently, Bighorn Brewing produces seven ales. The Big Horn Hefeweizen, a light, slightly hopped wheat, is closer to a true German-style Hefeweizen than most. Buttface Amber Ale, a medium-bodied, dark caramel-colored amber, is a well-balanced mix of malt and hops, with a decidedly fruity finish. Red Horn Red, Black Cat Honey Stout and Blewesberry, a blueberry Hefeweizen, are Bighorn's three other standard ales. A Belgian Wit and a malty, well-spiced Winter Ale have been the brewery's seasonals to date.

Proximity to Willamette University and Salem's historic district makes the Bighorn Brewing Company a natural draw for students and visitors alike. Future plans include two handles for cask-conditioned ales, several new seasonals, and distribution to area restaurants and pubs.

Cascade Microbrewery & Public Firehouse
3529 Fairview Industrial Drive SE
Salem, OR 97302
503/378-0737

The Cascade Microbrewery, with its antique firehouse gear, two 1915 Model T cars, player grand piano, larger-than-life stuffed toy Dalmatian, twinkling lights and bright red tables and chairs, is about the last thing a visitor would expect to find in an industrial park minutes from the Salem airport. Opened in 1995 by firefighter and homebrewer Tim Maronay, the brewery has become a quasi-museum of regional fire fighting history, as well as an alehouse serving many of the best Oregon craft brews.

Starting with 40 taps pouring beers from mostly small Oregon microbreweries, the Cascade Microbrewery then introduced its own ales to an enthusiastic crowd. Backdraught Ale, the favorite of both brewer and patrons, is a high alcohol, lightly hopped ale with plenty of malt flavors. Backdraught Bitter, a recent addition to Cascade's Firehouse Ales, is a hoppy, medium-amber ale, with a healthy balance of malt and hops. Cascade Wheat, a Hefeweizen-style ale, Ember Reizen, a mix of rye, wheat and barley malts, and a series of fruit-flavored wheat ales are Cascade Microbrewery's other standard brews.

The diverse offerings typical of an alehouse, combined with the unique flavors and character of its own ales, makes a stop at the Cascade Microbrewery a treat for any beer enthusiast. Ales from many of the best, smallest and most distant Oregon craft breweries are available here. Rather than distract patrons from Cascade's own fine ales, the selection provides both as an education and celebration of Pacific Northwest brewing.

Established: 1995

Hours: 11 am-midnight Monday-Friday, 11:30 am-midnight Saturday, 11:30 am-10 pm Sunday

Children: Yes

Food: Traditional pub fare

Entertainment: Board games, weekend acoustic musicians, televised sporting events

Smoking: No

Payment: Checks, Visa/MC

Takeout: Yes

Directions: From I-5, take exit 253 to route 22 West. Turn right on Madrona Avenue. Turn left onto Fairview Industrial Drive and turn right at first parking area. Brewery is visible from Madrona on left.

Mt. Angel Brewing Company

210 Monroe Street
Mt. Angel, OR 97362
503/845-9624

Established: 1995

Hours: 11 am-10 pm
Monday-Thursday, 11 am-11 pm Friday and
Saturday, 11 am-9 pm
Sunday

Children: Yes

Food: Extensive menu
with German emphasis;
all items cooked on wood
pellet grills

Entertainment: Acoustic
musicians

Smoking: No

Payment: Visa/MC, Am
Ex, Discover

Takeout: Yes

Directions: Take exit 271
off of I-5. Follow signs to
Woodburn and Mt. Angel.
Brewery is in the
middle of town
on the main
street of
Mt. Angel,
route 214.

Located in the richly historic town of Mt. Angel, the Mt. Angel Brewing Company is an integral part of the town's past and its future. Envisioned by its owners as a place where members of the local community could meet and celebrate, the company occupies a 100-year-old building (once a grain and potato storehouse).

The building is well-equipped for the many parties, banquets, meetings and receptions held there, with over 300 seats, two levels and three rooms filled with tables. Turn-of-the-century photographs of the town decorate the wall. While sampling the beer you may hear the peal of bells from the recently restored church tower (damaged during a recent earthquake).

Curt Gouverneur is a third generation brewer, taught by his father and grandmother. He is presently brewing four ales, including the Ale Mari, a German-style Hefeweizen, the Halo Pale, a lightly hopped ale with a strong fruity finish, the Angel Ale, an amber, and the Holy Grale, a roasted, fairly light-bodied porter. The names of the beers are quite appropriate for the town: Mt. Angel has strong Catholic roots and has been home to several religious institutions during its history, including both a men's and women's college, a convent and monastery. Mt. Angel also produces an outstanding root beer.

The town of Mt. Angel comes alive every year for Octoberfest, an event not to be missed. The Mt. Angel Brewing Company quickly sold out of its seasonal Strawberry Wheat last year, but plans to make it available in time for the next Octoberfest celebration.

Golden Valley Brewery Pub & Restaurant
980 E. 4th Street
McMinnville, OR 97128
503/472-2739

In 1993, Peter and Celia Kircher opened the Golden Valley Brewery and Pub, creating a place for family and friends to gather and reviving the tradition of brewing. The working-class town's brewing history dates back to 1878, when Anton Ahrens and W.R. Bachman opened the Ahrens Brewing Company.

The exposed timbers, high ceilings and copper brewing equipment visible from anywhere in the pub are the traits of the traditional warehouse-style brewpub. The Golden Valley Brewing Company enhances its historic 1921 building with a gorgeous antique bar, complete with intricate stained glass, and plenty of room for weekend blues and rock bands.

Golden Valley produces five standard ales, a root beer, and a variety of seasonal ales. Red Thistle Ale, its most popular brew, is a wonderful Scottish/Irish red with strong hop flavors. The Golden Valley Amber is a medium-colored, slightly bitter ale, with a malty flavor and subtle fruity finish. The Valley Weizen, a light wheat ale, and the Golden Ale, a mild-flavored, Pilsner-style ale, are the brewery's lighter offerings and would appeal to new craft beer enthusiasts. Golden Valley also brews a porter, and seasonals include a Nutbrown, stout, India Pale Ale, and Winter Ale.

In a region well-known for its wineries as well as its hops, the Golden Valley Brewing Company has established itself as a vintner of quality, local wines as well, producing a Pinot Noir and Chardonnay from Peter and Celia's vineyard just north of McMinnville. Be sure to get a bottle to take home before you wrap up your visit to Golden Valley.

Established: 1993

Hours: 11:30 am-11:30 pm Sunday-Thursday, 11:30 pm -12:30 am Friday and Saturday

Children: Yes (until 8:30 pm)

Red Thistle Ale

Wet your whistle – Grasp a thistle

Golden Valley Brewery

Food: Burgers, pizza, ribs, salads

Entertainment: Games, live blues and acoustic music on weekends

Smoking: Yes, in pub side, no in dining area

Payment: Checks, Visa/MC, Am Ex

Takeout: Yes

Directions: From Portland, take I-5 exit 294 to 99W to McMinnville. Follow signs to McMinnville (about 35 miles from Portland exit). Highway 99 splits into Adams going south and Baker going north in McMinnville. Take Adams to 3rd and turn left. Take 3rd through downtown until Johnson (streets are alphabetical). Turn left on Johnson. Brewery is on the left.

Saxer Brewing Company
4874 Lakeview Blvd.
Lake Oswego, OR 97035
503/699-9524

Established: 1993

Hours: 8 am-5 pm
Monday-Friday

Children: No

Food: No

Entertainment: No

Smoking: No

Payment: Checks

Takeout: Yes

Directions: I-5 to exit 290 (Lake Oswego/Durham). East on Boones Ferry to Jean Road. Right on Jean to Lakeview Blvd. and then right on Lakeview to brewery.

The Saxer Brewing Company, located in suburban Lake Oswego, is remarkably different than every other brewery in the Pacific Northwest. This is strictly a lagering operation – it produces no ales. Saxer beers can be found on grocery shelves in 29 states as well as Canada and Japan. The brewery recently won back-to-back Gold Medals at the Great American Beer Festival – in 1994 for best dark lager, and in 1995 for best Oktoberfest beer.

Housed in a large building just outside of Portland, Saxer is a high capacity bottling and kegging operation. A renovated tasting room complete with bar is available for private functions, and charitable organizations can used it free of charge. The brewery is directly behind the tasting room where rows and rows of conditioning tanks handle the time-intensive process of lagering Saxer's six standard beers. Unlike some ales which can be ready for consumption in approximately one week, lagers can take over two months to complete the conditioning process. The result is a smooth, easy-drinking beer with deep, well-rounded flavors.

Saxer's Lemon Lager, winner of many "People's Choice" awards at brew festivals, is a light, refreshing beer flavored with a hint of lemon. The 1994 Gold Medal winner, Three Finger Jack Hefedunkel, is an unfiltered, roasted dark red beer full of body. Three Finger Jack Amber, winner of the 1995 Octoberfest category, is a clean, well-balanced, malty beer very similar to traditional beers of Octoberfest. If you're seeking out the darkest beers, be sure to sample Three Finger Jack Stout.

The Willamette Week refers to Portland reverently as "Beervana." The Oregon Brewers Guild calls this city "Münich on the Willamette." Of the over 50 breweries and brewpubs in Oregon, more than one third are located in the Portland Metro area. Twenty of the 28 Oregon McMenamins establishments are found in and around Portland. The city is home to some of Oregon's largest and smallest microbreweries. The microbrewery revolution began in Oregon in 1984 with the opening of Bridgeport Brewing Company. The brewery began with a small "tasting room" modeled after those found in wineries. The open spaces, simple menu and variety of beers and serving styles have made Bridgeport a prototype for warehouse brewpubs.

The revolution might not have come so soon to Portland, however, if it were not for places like the Horse Brass Pub, located at 4534 SE Belmont. This pub, serving up the finest British and German beers to a crowd thirsting for full, rich flavor, was an inspiration to many brewers. It still serves as a showplace of the best of both Pacific Northwest and European lagers and ales.

Today, Portland boasts 16 breweries with nearly 40 brewpubs. McMenamins alone has 20 pubs, six of which brew. Four of these operations, Star Brewing, Saxer, Multnomah and Hair of the Dog, are exclusively breweries, supplying bottled and draft beer to local pubs and national markets.

Three of Oregon's largest microbreweries, Portland Brewing Company, Nor'Wester and Bridgeport, began in the Portland area. Oregon's smallest brewery, Philadelphia's Steaks & Hoagies, with an annual production of around 150 barrels, has been brewing in Portland since fall, 1994. And the opening of brewing operations in the Portland area has not stopped – McMenamins is renovating the historic Crystal Ballroom, and Beaverton, just south of Portland, will soon have a new brewpub. Rumors and plans of other new ventures will bring several more into the area.

There seems to be no end to the growing interest in microbrewed beer. Flavor, quality ingredients, higher alcohol content and local pride are some of the many reasons people are trying and switching to micros. With so much fine beer in the Portland area, however, is the market getting saturated? Consider that microbrews account for less than 2% of all beer sales in the United States. In the Portland area, that number is approaching 10%. Even in "Beervana," there is tremendous room for growth, as more and more beer drinkers discover the wonderful taste of craft brews.

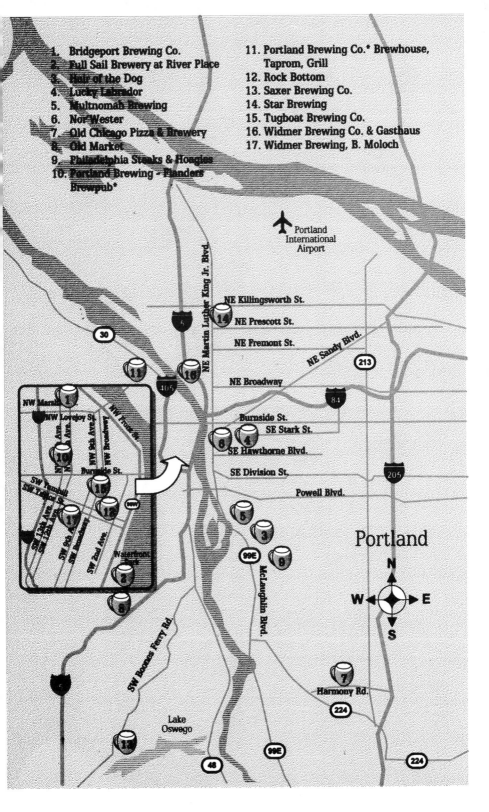

1. Bridgeport Brewing Co.
2. Full Sail Brewery at River Place
3. Hair of the Dog
4. Lucky Labrador
5. Multnomah Brewing
6. Nor'Wester
7. Old Chicago Pizza & Brewery
8. Old Market
9. Philadelphia Steaks & Hoagies
10. Portland Brewing - Flanders Brewpub*

11. Portland Brewing Co.* Brewhouse, Taprom, Grill
12. Rock Bottom
13. Saxer Brewing Co.
14. Star Brewing
15. Tugboat Brewing Co.
16. Widmer Brewing Co. & Gasthaus
17. Widmer Brewing, B. Moloch

Portland International Airport

NE Killingsworth St.
NE Prescott St.
NE Fremont St.
NE Sandy Blvd.
NE Broadway
Burnside St.
SE Stark St.
SE Hawthorne Blvd.
SE Division St.
Powell Blvd.

NE Martin Luther King Jr. Blvd.

NW Marsh
NW Lovejoy St.
N Ave.
NW 9th Ave.
Burnside St.
SW Yamhill
SW 17th St.
SW 13th Ave.
SW 12th St.
SW 8th Ave.
SW Broadway
SW 2nd Ave.
Waterfront Park
NW Front St.
NW Franklin Ave.

SW Boones Ferry Rd.

McLaughlin Blvd.

Harmony Rd.

Lake Oswego

Portland

N
W — E
S

Bridgeport Brewing Company
1313 NW Marshall Street
Portland, OR 97209
503/241-7179

Established: 1984

Hours: 2 pm-11 pm
Monday-Thursday, 2 pm-
midnight Friday,
noon-midnight Saturday,
1 pm-9 pm Sunday

Children: Yes

Food: Pizza, focaccia,
sausage sand-
wiches

Bridgeport Brewing Company, Oregon's oldest operating microbrewery, introduced
craft ales to the Portland area in 1984. Housed
in an impressive 100-year-old rope factory built of brick and timber in
Portland's historic Pearl District, the
brewery and pub have become a part
of the neighborhood.

Bridgeport has maintained its com-
mitment to producing outstanding
British-style ales as it has grown.
Its most popular offering, Blue
Heron Pale Ale, known as the
Bridgeport Pale Ale outside of
the Northwest, is a medium-bodied
amber bitter with a slightly fruity finish.
Bridgeport Nutbrown Ale, referred to as "The
Original," is currently available only in the pub.
Bridgeport also makes outstanding dark ales –
be sure to try the XX Stout and the Fremont
Porter, both wonderful renditions of the styles.

Entertainment:
Darts, live
music first
Thursday of each
month

Smoking: No

Payment: Checks,
Visa/MC

Takeout: Yes

The brewery's newest offerings are their Firkin
Beers. Firkins are nine-gallon British kegs used
to cask-condition beers. Bridgeport offers a full
range of cask-conditioned and bottle-condi-
tioned ales, allowing the natural carbonation
process and warmer temperatures to bring out
the subtle flavors and rich characteristics of
their ales.

Directions: From I-5
heading north to
Portland, take exit to I-
405 and then take the
Everett Street exit. Take
Everett to Marshall. Turn
right on Marshall.
Brewery is on the corner.
From I-5 heading south,
take exit to I-405 and
then take Everett Street
exit. Go two lights to
Everett and take a left.
Go to first light (14th)
and turn left. Head down
14th to Marshall.

A tour of the Bridgeport facility (weekends between 2 pm and 4 pm) allows the visitor to
explore the dark recesses of this magnificent
building. The timbers and floors are still soaked
with oils from the original rope factory. Outside
seating is available on the dock, with trains
passing only a few feet away. The smells and
tastes of thick, crunchy pizzas (the crusts are
made with unfermented beer wort) are an outstanding accompaniment to the ales.

Full Sail at River Place

0307 SW Montgomery
Portland OR 97201
503/220-1865

Full Sail at River Place in downtown Portland is a showcase for the Full Sail Brewing Company's extensive collection of ales and lagers. Though it represents only 4% of Full Sail's total brewing production, the River Place Pilsner Room is the source for many seasonals and specialty brews, and serves as the pilot brewery for the newest Full Sail releases.

The River Place Marina is a posh collection of shops, galleries and condos situated between Downtown Portland and the Willamette River. McCormick & Schmick's Harborside restaurant shares space with Full Sail in this building, offering an upscale menu, full bar, several guest taps and a complete selection of Full Sail ales and lagers, including two cask-conditioned ales. The restaurant, with its extensive woodwork, columns and two walls of floor-to-ceiling windows facing the river, encourages visitors to enjoy Full Sail's brews at a leisurely pace. Pilsner is always on tap, and many of Full Sail's seasonals find a home here while waiting for their turn in rotation. The Old Boardhead Barleywine Ale is also available here more regularly than Full Sail's Hood River facility.

A host of other Pacific Northwest micros are always on tap, mostly from the larger craft brewers. McCormick & Schmick's also features an extensive Northwest wine list and a full bar. Full Sail plans to offer a complete one day package, including tours of both Full Sail facilities, a tasting and dinner at McCormick & Schmick's, making it the perfect last stop on your tour of the Portland breweries.

Established: 1992

Hours: 11:30 am-closing Monday-Saturday, 10 am-closing, Sunday

Children: Yes

Food: Extensive, upscale restaurant menu

Entertainment: Television in the bar area

Smoking: Yes, in the bar area

Payment: Checks, Visa/MC, Am Ex, Discover

Takeout: No

Directions: From I-5 heading north in Portland, take Front Avenue exit. At first light turn right. At blinking red turn left. Brewery is just down the street. From I-5 heading south in Portland, take Morrison Bridge exit to City Center. Cross over bridge and take Front Street exit heading south. Turn left onto Market Street, then left at next light onto Montgomery. Brewery is just ahead on left.

Hair of the Dog Brewing Company
4509 SE 23rd
Portland, OR 97202
503/232-6585

Established: 1994

Hours: 9 am-4 pm
Monday-Friday

Children: Yes

Food: No

The Hair of the Dog Brewing Company fills a much-needed niche in American brewing, by producing gourmet brews on a par with some of the best Belgian and German breweries. Using a process unique in the US. the company has bottled small batches of wonderfully flavorful, high alcohol ales since 1994.

A tour of the brewery, located in a somewhat dilapidated warehouse in industrial southeast Portland, could possibly be one of the most educational beer-related experiences available in the Pacific Northwest. The two ales, Adambier and Golden Rose, are produced through an elaborate brewing and conditioning process, and are then refermented in the bottle through the addition of yeast and new beer, in a process known as krausening. The resulting ale can be stored at room temperature and allowed to age for years, with the taste mellowing and improving over time.

Adambier, recently awarded "Domestic Beer of the Year" by Malt Advocate, is the brewery's flagship ale. A revival of an old German-style, Adambier is a hearty, high alcohol ale with a high hop profile, yet is suprisingly smooth. Best served at room temperature and designed as a "sipping" ale, it is also the progenitor of two ales available only at the brewery. The Dog's other bottled offering, Golden Rose, inspired by the Belgian Tripel style, is a very fruity ale with a subtle hop flavor.

With its commitment to high quality and tradition, Hair of the Dog offers the beer enthusiast an educational experience, royal treatment for the palate and a wicked hang-over (the tongue-in-cheek inspiration for their name) for those foolish enough to think that the "Dog" is all bark and no bite.

Entertainment: No

Smoking: No

Payment: Checks

Takeout: Yes

Directions: From I-5 in Portland, take the Ross Island Bridge exit. Follow signs to Ross Island Bridge and cross over the Willamette River heading west. Take first right off the bridge to 99E south. Take Holgate exit and take Holgate to SE 26th. Turn right on Schiller. Turn right on SE 24th. Turn left on Pardee (gravel road). Turn right onto SE 23rd. Brewery is in the corner of the building on the left.

Lucky Labrador Brewing Company
915 SE Hawthorne Street
Portland, OR 97214
503/236-3555

The Lucky Labrador Brewing Company is housed in a huge, airy warehouse in southeast Portland. Despite the wall-sized Andrew Wyeth reproduction (Labrador appropriately included) opposite the enormous bar, this is a sparse and somewhat dark pub. However, weekends, standing-room only crowds quickly fill up the cavernous space, creating a giant party atmosphere.

The Lucky Labrador, with its wall of canine photos donated by patrons, is more than just a clever marketing gimmick. Since opening in 1994, the brewery has developed several outstanding ales. Hawthorne's Best Bitter, a dry hopped medium amber ale, is the current crowd favorite. Black Lab Stout, with a rich, roasted flavor and ample hops, has a loyal following and is often served cask-conditioned. Seasonals Scottish Holiday, a heavy, malty dark ale (available winters) and Quality Rye, a wonderful brew using malted rye (available summers), are worth the return trip. The brewery also serves a Kölsch-style Golden ale, a porter, an India Pale Ale and a red.

The company specializes in its own version of a bento (chicken or veggie), barbequed on the patio grill. Food is inexpensive and designed to complement the flow of Lucky Lab Ales. Though it's one of the least flashy or upscale of Portland's many brewpubs, well-crafted ales will make you glad you stopped by.

Established: 1994

Hours: 11 am-midnight Monday-Saturday, 1 m-10 pm Sunday

Children: Until 9 pm

Food: Limited pub menu

Entertainment: Darts and games available, acoustic musicians on weekends

Smoking: No, inside pub. Yes, on covered outdoor patio.

Payment: Checks, Visa, Am Ex, Discover

Takeout: Yes

Directions: From I-5 heading north, take the Hawthorne Blvd. exit. Head up Hawthorne towards 10th Avenue. Brewery is on left just before 10th.

Multnomah Brewing Company

1603 SE Pardee Street
Portland, OR 97202
503/236-3106

Established: 1993

Hours: Call for tours

Children: Yes

Food: No

Entertainment: No

Smoking: No

Payment: No retail sales

Takeout: No

Directions: From I-5 in Portland, take the Ross Island Bridge exit. Take 99E south for approximately one mile to the Holgate Blvd. exit. At the bottom of the hill turn right on 16th and right again on Pardee. Brewery is half way up the street on the right.

The Multnomah Brewing Company, hiding in the basement of a pink house off Holgate Boulevard, is easily physically the smallest microbrewery in the Pacific Northwest. Ducking and stooping is required – in some places the floor had to be lowered to squeeze in brewing equipment. A brewery tour is quick, primarily because there are just two rooms to visit.

From this small brewery, however, come five ales that grace the tap handles of many Portland area and Willamette Valley pubs. Figurehead Ale, the brewery's bestseller, is an amber-colored Pale Ale. Sauvie Island, a light golden Pale, offers both a heavy hop aroma and finish, due to added dry hopping in the kegs. Multnomah Brown, Multnomah Stout and a Special Bitter are the brewery's three other ales.

While a keg is always tapped and ready for tasting, you'll gain an even better appreciation for Multnomah Ales if you visit the Horse Brass Pub at 4534 SE Belmont in Portland. In addition to Multnomah Ales, Horse Brass offers over 25 draft ales, several cask-conditioned. Multnomah is currently maxed out at around 360 barrels a year. Brewer Jeff Hendryx plans a move and expansion and a boost in production in the near future. This will make the name and quality products of Multnomah Brewing Company available to a even greater number of enthusiastic drinkers.

Nor'Wester Public House
66 SE Morrison Street
Portland, OR 97214
503/232-9771

Established: 1993

Hours: 11 am-10 pm Monday-Wednesday, 11 am-11 pm Thursday-Saturday, 4 pm-10 pm Sunday

Children: Yes

Food: Limited pub menu

Entertainment: Darts, board games, live music on weekends

Smoking: No

Payment: Checks, Visa/MC

Takeout: Yes

The Nor'Wester brewpub, one of the first Pacific Northwest brewing operations financed by a public stock offering, was founded with the support of over 3,200 stockholders. The 50-barrel brewhouse, located under the busy Morrison Street Bridge, is the flagship brewery of the Willamette Valley Brewing Company, which is planning to open a series of breweries around the country over the next several years.

The actual pub takes up two very small rooms in the front of the red brick brewery. Seating is limited, and the weekend live music programs make it all but impossible to talk. Taking its name from the early non-native trappers and explorers to the Oregon Territory, the Nor'Wester brewpub, its logo and artwork reflect a rugged outdoor theme. The walls are decorated with antique skiing equipment, snow shoes and other equipment, as well as large outdoor murals.

Nor'Wester brews five standard ales and a winter seasonal. Three wheat ales include the pale, cloudy Hefeweizen; the darker, slightly roasted, award-winning Dunkel Weizen; and the assertively fruity Raspberry Weizen. The Nor'Wester Best Bitter, a deep copper-colored hoppy ale, and the Black Smith Porter, a dark, roasted, creamy porter, are the other two standard ales. Oregon's Grog, a Scottish-style dark and malty ale with a touch of raspberry, is the brewery's seasonal offering.

Directions: From I-5 north, take the OMSI exit and go to Water Street, then north to the brewpub. From I-5 south, take Burnside exit to Martin Luther King Blvd., then south to Stark Street. Turn right on Stark to Water Street. Turn right on Morrison and brewpub is one block down.

Old Chicago

11211 SE 82nd Avenue
Clackamas, OR 97015
503/655-1941

The Clackamas Old Chicago (part of the Rock Bottom empire of restaurants and breweries) is currently the only one in the country that brews its own beer. With over 110 other beers offered by the restaurant, the fact that it does brew might seem a little strange. But the trio of very tasty ales brewed in the small, four-barrel brewhouse consistently outsells the others.

The building is located in a suburban mall surrounded by spacious parking lots. First impressions from the outside, however, do not do the restaurant justice. This is actually a warm, inviting space filled with cozy wooden booths and tables and decorated with dozens of colorful flags hanging from the ceiling, as well as various Chicago baseball memorabilia. It's the perfect place to spend a chilly, rainy day playing pool, eating deep-dish pizza or watching the game.

Old Chicago brews three standard ales and variety of seasonals. Northern Sun Golden Ale, the local favorite, is a light-bodied, very drinkable, amber-colored ale. Wrigley Red, a sweet, malty flavored red ale, and Miles Davis Stout, a medium-bodied dark ale with a lightly roasted flavor, are the brewery's two other offerings. Winter Ale, Summer Wheat and Raspberry Porter make up the seasonals. Old Chicago also runs a club for the insatiable regulars who may want to try all of the 110 beers available at the restaurant. The "Hall of Foamers" is reserved for those mighty few who eventually sample all of the many ales, and members receive prizes

Established: 1994

Hours: 11 am to 2 am daily

Children: Yes

Food: Famous for their Chicago-style pizza

Entertainment: Pool, television

Smoking: No

Payment: Checks, Visa/MC, Am Ex, Diners

Takeout: Yes

Directions: I-5 to I-205 to the 82nd Street exit. Take 82nd about four miles to brewery. Brewery is on the left.

The Old Market Pub & Brewery

6959 SW Multnomah Boulevard
Portland, OR 97223
503/244-0450

The two-mile trip down the narrow and picturesque Multnomah Blvd. to the Old Market Pub & Brewery will make you forget that downtown Portland is just minutes away. However, the bustling Old Market Pub is anything but quiet.

The pub is comprised of a large, open room filled with a long wooden bar, booths and tables in front, and a slightly smaller room with a big-screen TV that is also used for private parties. A third room in back provides ample space for pool tables and shuffleboard. Formerly the Comella and Sons Market (hence the name), the Old Market Pub has incorporated much of the theme and decor of a greengrocer's shop. Giant murals of fruit labels decorate the walls, and what were once hanging scales now make great planters. There are murals throughout the building, including the pool room, where the walls show silhouettes of drinkers complete with half empty pint glasses.

The brewery produces a range of ales including a light Pale Ale, the very hoppy Dr. Dan's Backward Bitter, Mr. Toad's Red Ale – the best of the Old Market's offerings, a wheat ale, porter and a rather dry stout. Seasonals have included a Brown Ale and a jalapeño-spiced Pale Ale. A variety of other regional micros are available as well.

The menu is almost as expansive as the building. Five calzones, six nacho platters, nine burgers, and 10 pizzas are just the beginning of the Old Market offerings. This remarkable pub is definitely a required stop for microbrewing enthusiasts looking for atmosphere as well as quality craft ales.

Established: 1994

Hours: 11 am-midnight Monday-Thursday, 11 am-1 am Friday, noon-1 am Saturday, noon-midnight Sunday

Children: Yes

Food: Extensive pub menu including pizzas and calzones

Entertainment: Pool, televised sporting events

Smoking: No

Payment: Checks, Visa/MC, Am Ex

Takeout: Yes

Directions: From I-5 just south of Portland, take the Multnomah Blvd. exit. Pub is two miles on the right at Multnomah and 69th.

The Old Market Pub & Brewery

Philadelphia's Steaks & Hoagies

6410 SE Milwaukie Avenue
Portland, OR 97202
503/239-8544

Established: 1994

Hours: 9 am-9 pm daily

Children: Yes

Food: Philadelphia cheese steaks and hoagies

Entertainment: Pools, television, video poker

Smoking: No

Payment: Checks

Takeout: Yes

Philadelphia's Steaks & Hoagies in the Milwaukie area is an oasis for both visitors from the East Coast and transplants to the Pacific Northwest. Owner Steve Moore, originally from the Philly area, has successfully combined the mouth-watering tastes of Philadelphia cheese steaks and hoagies with the creativity and flavors of Oregon's smallest microbrewery.

Despite being an integrated suburb community just south of Portland, the Milwaukie area has that small-town feel. Storefronts and buildings have changed little in the past 30 years. Philadelphia's Steaks & Hoagies adds a bit of nostalgia and Philly style and, of course, a variety of cheese steaks and hoagies. A collection of posters, maps, sports memorabilia and a Philadelphia skyline mural painted around the walls of the restaurant complete the theme.

Directions:
Take the Ross Island Bridge exit from I-5 in Portland. Cross over bridge and take first right onto 99E. Take 99E south to Milwaukie Avenue. Go right on Milwaukie about 12 blocks. Pub is on the left across the street from a grocery store.

In 1994, Moore added a brewing operation, one of the smallest in Oregon. Despite limited capacity, Philadelphia's produces seven standard ales and five seasonals. Creativity is the watchword at this brewery, and every batch is subject to brewer's fancy. Double Hopped Eagle Ale, an extra hoppy India Pale Ale, is the perfect example. The Eagle Ale is darker than most India Pale Ale's due to the addition of some chocolate and Munich malts. Three porter variations – Broad Street Porter, South Street Porter, and Blackberry Porter – all offer something of interest to the dark ale enthusiast. The Ginger Beer, with a wheat base and the added zing of fresh ginger, is a must try. The brewery also produces a Hefeweizen, golden, red, brown and stout.

Portland Brewing Company/ Flanders Street Brewpub
1339 NW Flanders Street
Portland, OR 97209
503/222-5910

Now a major regional craft brewery, the Portland Brewing Company was born of humbler beginnings in the Flanders Street Brewpub. While heavy-production brewing is now handled at the brewhouse on NW 31st, Flanders Street is the original and, for the fiercely loyal clientele, only true Portland Brewing Company.

Flanders Street was one of the forces heralding the microbrewing renaissance in Portland and the Pacific Northwest. The beautiful two-story brewery, visible from the pub, is still used to produce Portland Brewing's specialty beers and pilot batches. With luck, you'll find on-tap offerings of Tartan Scottish Ale, a wonderfully sweet, malty ale, Portland Brown, a porter-like dark with a hint of roasted flavors, or Portland Stout, a thick and creamy stout with well-balanced chocolate and roasted characteristics.

This friendly and cozy pub located in the historic Pearl District is almost holy ground for its long-time regulars. The forest green curtains strung around the top of the two-story walls, the small, dark wooden tables and a glass-enclosed display of brewing memorabilia from turn-of-the-century Portland create an atmosphere thick with old-world comforts. Come Tuesday nights to catch a glimpse of the heart and soul of the pub, as the crusty regulars down MacTarnahan's Ale and an impromptu darts tournament transfixes the crowd. Weekends feature Dixieland and jazz, with music filling the pub from the second floor balcony stage. A visit to the Flanders Street Brewpub is a must for any craft brewing enthusiast.

Established: 1986

Hours: 11:30 am-11 pm Monday-Thursday, noon-midnight Friday and Saturday, 1 pm-7 pm Sunday

Children: Yes

Food: Sandwiches

Entertainment: Darts, televised sports, live music

Smoking: No

Payment: Visa/MC

Takeout: No

Directions: From I-5 in Portland, take I-405 to Everett Street exit. Turn left on 14th, then right on Flanders. Brewery is second building on left.

Oregon 51

Portland Brewing Company

2730 NW 31st Avenue
Portland, OR 97210
503/228-5269

Established: 1993

Hours: 11 am-10 pm
Monday-Thursday, 11 am-
midnight Friday and
Saturday, noon-7:30pm
Sunday

Children: Yes

Food: Full pub-style menu
with German overtones

Entertainment: Live
music on weekends

Smoking: No

Payment:
Checks,
Visa/MC

Takeout:
Yes

Directions:
From I-5
North, take Exit
302B to Highway 30.
Take a left on Nicolai.
Turn right on 26th. 26th
becomes Industrial
Street. Brewery is on the
corner of Industrial and
31st.

The new Portland Brewing Company brewery and pub, built with the financial support of over 5,500 shareholders, is an extraordinary showcase of beers and brewing. Situated in Portland's industrial Northwest district, the massive, multi-story building will catch a first-time visitor completely by surprise. The front room is completely taken up by two 140-barrel copper brewing kettles, brought to Portland from the centuries-old Sixenbrau Brewery in Bavaria.

Decorated in a fairly consistent Bavarian style, the pub includes large murals, stunning multi-handled beer towers and a collection of antique beer steins beside the fireplace. The tastes and smells of a German-influenced kitchen permeate the air. The beers, in contrast to the decor, favor styles from the British Isles and America. Pub favorite is the Oregon Honey Beer, a pale, light-bodied ale with only a hint of honey flavor and a dry finish. MacTarnahan's Ale, a copper-colored, Scottish-style ale, has a rich caramel flavor and smooth finish. Wheat Berry Brew, a wheat ale with the added flavor of Oregon marionberries, is a summer favorite. Portland Brewing Company's latest bottled offering, the Haystack Black, is a reddish-brown ale with a satisfying blend of roasted and chocolate malts.

The brewery has grown from an annual production of around 5,000 barrels in 1991 to over 40,000 barrels. Tours of this state-of-the-art, 100,000-barrel capacity brewing operation are conducted Saturdays every hour from 1 pm to 5 pm. Visitors can also collect a wealth of printed information about the brewery, buy a shirt or cap and learn about becoming a shareholder in this fast-growing and quality brewery.

Rock Bottom Brewery

210 SW Morrison Street
Portland, OR 97204
503/796-2739

Established: 1994

Hours: 11 am-1 am
Monday-Saturday, 11 am-
midnight Sunday

Children: Yes

Food: Upscale pub fare

Entertainment: Pool, televised sports, weekend
musicians

Smoking: Yes, in bar area

Payment: Checks,
Visa/MC, Am Ex, Diners
Club

Takeout: Yes

Directions: From I-5 in
Portland, take the
Morrison Bridge exit
heading to downtown
Portland. Go forward off
the bridge to 3rd and
turn left. Turn left onto
Morrison. Brewery is on
the right side at 2nd and
Morrison.

This Rock Bottom Brewery is the brewery chain's first foray into the Pacific Northwest. The company started in Boulder, Colorado, in 1991, and now includes breweries in cities such as Chicago and Denver.

Characterizing itself as a "restaurant that brews beer," Portland's Rock Bottom takes advantage of its downtown location, serving as a lunch-time spot for businesses, a place to stop before or after a basketball game, theater or music event, and a destination for restaurant and microbrewery enthusiasts. The brewery boasts five standards and a variety of seasonals. A bit tamer than most Pacific Northwest ales, the Rock Bottom downplays the strong hop flavors popular in this region. The White Pelican Pale Ale, one of its most popular drinks, is the hoppiest of the Rock Bottom offerings, with a light honey color and a fairly bitter finish. Falcon Red Ale, a medium-bodied, malty red, is a smooth, darker ale, while the Black Seal Stout, served warm with very little carbonation, will appeal to those who find most stouts too roasted or heavy.

The Rock Bottom Restaurant is an expansive, bustling, crowded place. The second floor is devoted almost entirely to pool tables and the brewery, with the fermenters and conditioning tanks visible from the bar area. Though it has the feel of a big city restaurant, it also offers the qualities and temptations of an inhouse microbrewery.

BIG HORN NUT BROWN ALE

DOWNTOWN
THE
ROCK BOTTOM
BREWERY
PORTLAND

Star Brewing Company

5231 NE Martin Luther King Jr. Blvd.
Portland, OR 97211
503/282-6003

Established: 1993

Hours: 8 am-5 pm
Monday-Friday

Children: No

Food: No

Entertainment: No

Smoking: No

Payment: Checks

Takeout: Yes

Directions: From I-5 in
Portland, take the
Killingsworth exit. Turn
east onto Killingsworth
(right if coming from the
south, left if from the
north) and go
about 20
blocks to
NE Martin
Luther King
Blvd. Turn
right on MLK
Blvd. Brewery
is one block
down on the
right.

Don't expect bells and whistles at Star Brewing Company. One of the first things that comes to mind when you walk into the brewery, housed in a garage in the heart of northeast Portland, is that it should really be in a larger building. A recent expansion and purchase of Full Sail's old equipment has pushed this facility to the limit. Brewers here squirm under and squeeze between tanks, perch on platforms above the kettle and generally make use of every inch of space.

The brewery is cramped and loud, cold in winter and hot in summer. And it definitely smells like beer. Even though Star will probably be required to move to larger quarters to keep up with demand for its ales, there is an excitement and down-to-earth feel that comes from a visit to this brewery.

Star brews a variety of ales, ranging from traditional favorites to modern hybrids. The most popular ale is a Raspberry Wheat, while the provocative Black Cherry Stout and Pineapple Ale both take the current interest in fruited ales to something of an extreme. The Star Hop Gold Ale, the flagship product of the original Star Brewery in Vancouver, Washington, has been revived 100 years later with the addition of rye to the base recipe.

The ales are creative, unique and range from smooth and refreshing to big and complex. A visit to Star is a welcome contrast to the many polished, glass-encased breweries found today and a must for any individual who wants to get a feel for the tremendous work behind the magical brewing process.

Tugboat Brewing Company
711 SW Ankeny Street
Portland, OR 97204
503/226-2508

Unassuming as brewpubs go – tucked down an alley off Broadway in downtown Portland – the Tugboat is frequented by faithful regulars, the city's bicycle messenger fleet, and the slightly baffled visitor in search of Portland's most eclectic brewing operation.

Somewhere between the dark mustard paint and the pickle barrels holding a vast array of beers is the true nature of the company. The owners and employees of the Tugboat are out to have fun. To date, the brewery has turned out more than 50 styles of beers. While it is unlikely the same brews are on tap at every visit, Russian Imperial Stout, English Brown, India Pale Ale and an Alt are some of the most stable offerings. Root beer, sarsaparilla and other sodas are also brewed in house.

A limited and affordable menu of burritos, nachos and garden burgers cater to the tastes of Tugboat's regular customers. The art work decorating the walls is for sale, and old copies of National Geographic or yesterday's paper are likely to be scattered on several tables, creating a comfortable, lived-in atmosphere.

The brewpub is at its best weekend evenings, when live blues and folk music often blends into free-for-all jams, and anyone with a bit of talent (or possibly without) can add his or her own sounds to the on-going music. The Tugboat brews under a similar philosophy – experimentation, group input and a bit of recklessness are just as important as the yeast, malt, and hops.

Established: 1993

Hours: Noon-midnight Monday-Friday, 3 pm-1 am Saturday, 3 pm to 11 pm Sunday

Children: Yes

Food: Small vegetarian menu

Entertainment: Lots of live music

Smoking: Yes

Payment: Cash only

Takeout: No

Directions: From I-5 in Portland, take exit 301 to the Burnside Bridge to downtown Portland. Cross river and take Burnside to Broadway. Turn left on Broadway. Tugboat is located just down Ankeny, the first street (almost an alley) on the right.

Widmer Brewing Company

B. Moloch/Heathman Bakery & Pub
901 SW Salmon Street
Portland, OR 97205
503/227-5700

Established: 1987

Hours: 7 am-11 pm daily

Children: Yes

Food: Wood-fired pizza, seafood specialties, salads

Entertainment: Television

Smoking: No

Payment: Checks, all major credit cards

Takeout: No

Directions: I-5 northbound in Portland to I-405 north. Take Salmon Street exit. Take Salmon to 9th. Brewery and pub is on northwest corner.

The B. Moloch/Heathman Pub is the result of a collaboration begun in 1987 between Widmer Brewing and the Heathman Bakery & Pub. Widmer is the brewery, visible behind the bar and from the outside of the building. The heavenly wood-fired pizzas, fresh-baked breads, pastas and seafood dishes comprise the bakery. The blending of the two is an exciting union – Widmer ales flavor many of the regionally inspired entrees, while the choice of foods is often determined by what will go best with the various Widmer ales.

The pub is graced by seven life-size caricatures painted in oils by B. Moloch. The brewery produces the B. Moloch Ur-Alt, Widmer's flagship ale and the house ale of the Heathman. The Ur-Alt is a German-styled ale with a rich copper color and a lingering hop flavor. The brewery, with an annual capacity of 2,500 barrels, now serves as Widmer's pilot brewery, as well as the location for the brewing of several of the Widmer seasonals.

The wonderful downtown location is a draw for shoppers and tourists, as well as those in need of a hip business lunch spot. In addition to offering a complete line of Widmer ales, the Heathman offers an excellent selection of Pacific Northwest brews. Wintertime visits may well be the best for beer enthusiasts, when the variety of seasonal winter ales on tap help cast out the damp and chill of Portland's rainy season.

Widmer Brewing & Gasthaus
955 N. Russell Street
Portland, OR 97227
503/281-3333

Widmer brothers Kurt and Rob, with their pioneering German-inspired brewing, have had a tremendous impact on the growing popularity of microbrews over the past decade. The Widmer Brewing Company is known throughout the Pacific Northwest and beyond for its amazingly popular Hefeweizen. This number one draft micro in the Pacific Northwest accounts for over 90% of the brewery's total production.

The new brewery and bottling operation and the Widmer Gasthaus (literally "guest house") in northeast Portland serve as the nucleus for the company's empire. The Gasthaus, a beautifully restored historic brick and wooden building, offers most of the brews on tap, complemented by a German-influenced menu with a Northwest flair. Visible behind glass windows is the original Gasthaus brewery. The new, greatly expanded brewery is just across the street and also holds Widmer's new bottling line. Beer passes beneath the street from each brewery – to the Gasthaus for kegging, across the street for bottling.

The brewery specializes in German-styled ales. Hefeweizen, Dunkelweizen and the hoppy Widmer Alt are all Americanized versions of classic German beers. The Doppelbock, Bock and Oktoberfest are found at the Gasthaus and on draft seasonally. The new brewing facility marks a departure for Widmer brothers as they throw themselves into the fiercely-competitive bottled market. If their success in producing high-quality draft beers is any indication, however, expect to see Widmer bottles showing up in markets all over the country.

Established: 1984

Hours: 11 am-11 pm Monday-Thursday and Sunday, 11 am-1 am Friday and Saturday

Children: Yes

Food: Extensive German-styled menu

Entertainment: Beer Garden with live entertainment in summer

Smoking: No

Payment: Checks, Visa/MC

Takeout: Yes

Directions: From I-5 northbound in Portland, take Weidler exit and turn left on Broadway. Turn right on to Interstate, then right on Russell. From I-5 southbound, take the Coliseum exit and turn right on Broadway. Turn on Interstate and right on Russell.

McMenamins Edgefield Brewery

2126 SW Halsey Street
Troutdale, OR 97060
800/669-8610

Established: 1990

Hours: Something is always happening at Edgefield from 7 am to 1 am daily

Children: Yes

Food: Upscale menu in restaurant; burgers and fries at the pub

Entertainment: Movie theater, live music, seasonal events

If there is a heaven for microbrew lovers this is it. Edgefield operates a bed and breakfast, a winery, brewery, pub, movie theater, upscale restaurant and much, much more, all from a picturesque, fully-restored 1911 County Poor Farm. Don't believe any of the exaggerated tales people will tell you about the pace. An actual visit is even better.

The best way to enjoy Edgefield is to stay overnight. There are over 100 bed and breakfast rooms available every night of the year. The hundreds of hand-painted murals and portraits covering the hallways and bedroom walls depict the various stages of the place's history, including its stint as an operating poor farm and its later incarnation as a nursing home.

McMenamins wines and ales are available in the downstairs Black Rabbit Restaurant and Bar. If you enjoy mouth-watering meals served in an elegant setting make dinner at the Black Rabbit a must before you head over to the Power Station Pub and Theater for late-evening fun. For more casual fare, the Pub serves burgers, salads and the famous McMenamins french fries. It also houses a movie theater. Bring a pint of Hammerhead or Ruby into the theater, sit back and relax.

Before you leave, take a peek at the brewery, which serves as the main brewery for McMenamins and produces Terminator Stout, Black Rabbit Porter, Bagdad Golden and other standard McMenamins ales for several of the company's Oregon pubs. If you have time, tour the Edgefield Gardens, vineyard or the Corcoran Glassworks. Then head up the Columbia Gorge to the spectacular waterfalls, or back into Portland to visit some of the other McMenamins pubs and breweries.

Smoking: No

Payment: Checks, all major credit cards

Takeout: Yes

Directions: From I-84 east from Portland, take exit 16A. Follow 238th. Drive south to first light and turn left on Halsey. Go 1/2 mile, Edgefield is on the right.

Big Horse Brewing Company
115 State Street
Hood River, OR 97031
503/386-4411

The Big Horse Brewing Company is the latest in a series of great ideas from owner and brewer Randy Orzeck. In 1987, Orzeck opened Horsefeathers, a restaurant and bar, and later launched a successful pasta business now distributing to Portland and other Oregon markets. Deciding to start a brewery in Full Sail Brewing's hometown seemed liked the next logical venture.

In 1995, Horsefeathers changed its name to the Big Horse Brewing Company, and the brewery was launched. The company currently produces four standards and four seasonals, much to the delight of Hood River natives and Columbia Gorge tourists and wind surfers. Pub favorites Night Mare Russian Imperial Stout, a well-balanced, full-bodied stout, and the lightly-hopped Pale Rider India Pale Ale, provide something for both the recent convert and the seasoned craft brew enthusiast. The seasonal Scotch Ale, a smooth, high-alcohol, darker ale, the Chompin Bitters Extra Special Bitter and the Branded Black Porter are also well worth a try.

The three-story pub is built right into the hillside that climbs toward snow capped Mt. Hood. The brewery is located on the ground floor and is visible from the street. On the second and third floors, wooden decks extend the pub and restaurant outdoors. A variety of games, televised sporting events, darts and summertime horseshoes are available for those not enjoying the beautiful setting. Visitors can sample Big Horse ales while admiring the Columbia River and surrounding cliffs, mountains and waterfalls.

Established: 1995

Hours: 4 pm-11 pm Thursday and Friday, 11:30 am-11 pm Saturday, 11:30 am-9 pm Sunday

Children: Yes

Food: Lunch and dinner menu, including gourmet burgers, pastas, clam chowder

Entertainment: Pool, darts, horseshoes, board games, televised sports, live music

Smoking: No

Payment: Checks, Visa/MC

Takeout: Yes

Directions: From I-84, take exit 63 for Hood River City Center. Take 2nd Avenue right until it deadends at State Street. Brewery is impossible to miss.

Full Sail-Hood River
506 Columbia Street
Hood River, OR 97031
503/386-2281

Established: 1987

Hours: Summer: noon-8 pm daily; Winter: noon-8 pm Thursday-Sunday

Children: Until 7 pm

Food: Bar snacks, nachos

Entertainment: Board games

Smoking: No

Payment: Checks

Takeout: Yes

Directions: From I-84, take exit 63 to Hood River City Center. Turn right from exit heading into town. Turn right on Cascade Street. Take a right on 5th. 5th dead-ends into Columbia at the Full Sail Brewing Company building.

Full Sail Brewing Company, the largest craft bottler in Oregon, began in a small building overlooking the Columbia River in downtown Hood River. Recent expansion has enlarged the building tremendously and boosted Full Sail's annual capacity to around 100,000 barrels a year. Still a small operation by commercial beer standards, the brewery has become a giant among craft breweries.

While many of Full Sail's beers are bottled and available throughout the Pacific Northwest and beyond, a visit to the Hood River brewing facility is well worth the trip. Staring down into a two-story kettle, watching the machinery crank out thousands of bottles of beer, and walking beneath the giant fermenters are just some of the grand-scale features of the hourly tours conducted every day (Thursday through Sunday in winter).

Don't miss a trip to the pub, where you can sample many of the ales. It's housed in the original portion of the building and usually has eight of the 14 beers on tap. The Full Sail Nutbrown, India Pale, Top Sail Porter or Full Sail Extra Special Bitter (the newest bottled Full Sail ale) are just a few of the ales offered. The company also brews several lagers, including the Full Sail Pilsner, Maibock, Mercator Dopplebock and Octoberfest, a malty Bavarian- style lager.

The pub, which is a simple room with few tables, is usually filled year-round with Hood River natives and visitors to the magnificent Columbia Gorge region. Summers, folks sit on the outdoor patio overlooking Columbia River and watch the wind surfers. In winter, the rustic wood-burning stove keeps out the chill of winter rain.

Mt. Hood Brewing Company

87304 Government Camp Loop
Government Camp, OR 97028
503/272-3724

Established: 1992

Hours: Noon-10 pm daily

Children: Yes

Food: Pizza, sandwiches, entrees, salads

Entertainment: Board games

Smoking: No

Payment: Checks, Visa/MC, Am Ex

Takeout: No

Directions: I-5 North to Portland, take exit 288 to I-205. Take Gresham exit to Highway 26 east. Take first Government Camp exit (45 miles from Gresham). Brewery is visible from the exit on the right side of the road.

Tucked under Oregon's highest peak on the edge of Government Camp is the Mt. Hood Brewing Company, the ideal watering hole for visitors drawn to the beauty and adventure of Mt. Hood.

While appropriately named for its mountain location, the brewery actually takes its name from the original Mt. Hood Brewing Company, which operated from 1905 to 1913 in Portland. The current brewery produces four standards and two seasonals, offered both at the Mt. Hood Brew Pub and many Portland and Willamette Valley restaurants and taverns. The popular Ice Axe India Pale Ale is wonderfully smooth, rich and hoppy. Pinnacle Extra Special Bitter, always cask-conditioned, will also appeal to hop enthusiasts. Hogsback Oatmeal Stout is strong and thick, with a dominant roasted flavor. Seasonals Southside Light Session Ale, a summer wheat, and Pittock Wee Heavy, a winter-released barleywine-style Scotch ale, are well suited to the needs of seasonal visitors.

Decorated in a rustic fly fishing and skiing motif with the brewhouse visible from the restaurant, the Mt. Hood Brewing Company building has a ski lodge atmosphere well-suited to its location. Whether you're here for fishing, hiking, climbing or skiing, a trip to the Mt. Hood Brewing Company is the perfect end to a long, satisfying day.

Seventh Street Brew House/ Cascade Lakes Brewing Company
855 SW 7th Street
Redmond, OR 97756
541/923-1795

There's just one brewpub in the small town of Redmond, but it's definitely worth the stop. The newly opened Seventh Street Brew House is the tasting grounds for the Cascade Lakes Brewing Company, Redmond's first and only brewery.

In less than 1,300 square feet, the Brew House has managed to fit a brewery for cask-conditioned ales, a bar, an eating area and room for entertainment. In the warmer months, tables, chairs and live music are pushed out to an expansive deck, doubling the space. It's possible even to get a little exercise by joining in a friendly game of volleyball. The pub comes with its own court.

Between the entertainment and the extensive list of tasty beers, it's easy to spend an entire afternoon at this pub. Locals rave about the Red Rooster Ale, but based on distribution outside of Redmond, Monkey Face Porter is also in demand. Other offerings include a Blackberry Kölsch, Grizzly Mountain Stout and the latest, Angus MacDougal's Scotts Ale, named after the brewer's great, great, great grandfather. In the summer, the brewery also produces Bandits Best Bitter, named after the local semi-pro baseball team.

Established: 1995

Hours: 11 am-10 pm Monday-Thursday, 11 am-midnight Friday and Saturday, 11 am-9 pm Sunday

Children: Yes

Food: Simple pub fare

Entertainment: Pub has live music throughout the year

Smoking: No, inside. Yes, on deck

Payment: Checks, Visa/MC

Takeout: Yes

Directions: To find the pub, take Highway 126 (Highland) to 7th Street. Turn right on 7th Street. Pub is across the street from the fairgrounds.

Seventh Street Brew House Cascade Lakes Brewing Company

Bend Brewing Company

1019 NW Brooks Street
Bend, OR 97701
541/383-1599

Old town Bend is like entering a Hollywood Western set – rustic, quaint and somewhat unreal. But inside Bend's newest brewpub, the cowboys give way to tired skiers, golfers or families just back from a long day of rafting.

Bend Brewing is more upscale than its friendly competitor, Deschutes Brewing Company (see page 64), just up the road, but the atmosphere is still relaxed and comfortable. Large windows offer a pleasant view of the park and the Deschutes River. Antique tables and chairs possibly once gracing an old English pub are scattered about the main dining and bar area. During warmer months, outdoor seating is available.

The brewery's beers are mostly traditional in style. Outback Old Ale is the brewery's strong ale and house favorite. Skyliner Stout and Elk Lake India Pale Ale are usually on the menu. Seasonal beers have included Paulina Pilsner, a tasty Sasquach Scotch Ale, and Downtown Brown Ale.

Bend Brewing prides itself not only on its fine hand-crafted beers, but also on its broad menu of deliciously prepared foods, including pizza, fish, pasta dishes, burritos, and burgers. The daily specials are also tantalizing to the palate.

Established: 1995

Hours:
11 am-midnight daily

Children: Yes

Food: Yes

Entertainment: Regular televised sporting events

Smoking: No

Payment: Checks, Visa/MC

Takeout: Yes

Directions: Head west on Greenwood from U.S. 97. Take a left on Brooks Street.

Deschutes Brewing Company
1044 NW Bond Street
Bend, OR 97701
541/382-9242

One of the most successful microbreweries in the state is the Deschutes Brewery, located in Bend, a town famous for its outstanding recreational opportunities.

This brewery has thrived since it first opened in 1988. It's a comfortable and contagiously friendly place. You'll soon find yourself swapping ski stories with the bartender while anxiously waiting for your hand-pumped beer.

Deschutes is best known for its Black Butte Porter, the best-selling porter in Oregon. It is also the only mircobrewery in the region to use whole hops in the brewing process. The head brewer claims this brings out a better-bodied beer and, from the way it's selling, it appears many others agree!

Mainstays include Cascade Golden, sweet with a fabulous burst of flavors, Bond Street Brown ale, Obsidian Stout, a Guinness-style stout with a thick cream top, and Bachelor Bitter, a local favorite. Don't miss the Jubelale, made special for the holiday season and on tap throughout the winter.

Deschutes' great beer is accompanied by an expansive menu offering pub-style food, soups, salads, sandwiches and pie for dessert. Kids can do their own sampling of homemade root beer or ginger ale.

Mt. Bachelor ski resort is just a short ride from town, the raging Deschutes River offers rafters and kayakers a thrilling course, and Smith Rock State Park offers some of the best rock climbing in the world. What could be better than a stop at Deschutes Brewery to finish off the day?

Established: 1988

Hours: 11 am -11:30pm Monday-Thursday, 11 am-12:30 am Friday and Saturday, 11 am-10 pm Sunday

Children: Yes

Food: Standard pub fare

Entertainment: Basket o' Tips, acoustic musicians on the weekends, televised sporting events

Smoking: No

Takeout: Yes

Payment: Checks, Visa/MC

Directions: From Highway 97, go west on Franklin to Bond. Right onto Bond. The brewery is 2½ blocks on the right.

Blue Mountain Brewing, LaGrande, OR 541/963-5426

Blue Mt. Brewing, the first brewing company to open in far eastern Oregon, is currently producing a Kölsch-style ale and a Weizen for a few draft accounts in the local area. The owners plan to open a tasting room or brewpub soon in the LaGrande area, but until then zoning laws prohibit the operation from accommodating visitors.

Osprey Ale Brewpub, 404 East Main Street, Medford, OR 541/734-4808

Owners Larry and Barbara Bruce are opening Medford's first brewpub at 404 E. Main. Sandwiches and appetizers will accompany several different ales including a bitter, stout, golden and pale. Osprey Ale Brewpub will be open Tuesday through Thursday from 4 pm to midnight and 4 pm to 1 am Friday and Saturday.

Pelican Pub & Brewery, 33180 Cape Kiwanda Drive, Pacific City, OR 503/965-7779

The northern Oregon Coast's first brewpub will be the Pacific City Brewing Company, located just a short walk from the beach at Cape Kiwanda in Pacific City. Emphasizing "American" style ales and lagers, brewer Darren Welch is planning to offer a Cream Ale, an American Brown, as well as a pilsner and Scottish-style amber. The pub will serve wood-fired pizzas, fish and chips and traditional pub fare.

Timberland Brewing Company, 5000 Crown Street, Charleston, OR 541/888-8230

The Timberland Brewing Company plans to distribute draft ales and bottled beer to the southern and central Oregon Coast region. Owner Fred Linneman intends to add a tasting room and retail store to the brewery located in the woods just outside of Charleston. Brews include a pale ale, amber, Weizen and at least one darker ale. The Charleston area is one of the most spectacular stops on the Oregon Coast and a perfect location for a brewery. Timberland joins nearby Bank Brewing Company in Coos Bay and Bandon Brewing Company in Bandon in a coastal brewery boom.

McMenamins Pubs & Breweries –
A Neighborhood Place for Family & Friends

In the Pacific Northwest, McMenamins breweries and pubs are as familiar and enjoyed as the forests for which the region is famous. In the early 1980s, Portland brothers Mike and Brian McMenamin saw the potential for opening a brewpub in the already draft-crazed beer market of Oregon. Little did they dream that without so much as writing a business plan, they would one day be operating a privately held, multi-million dollar company of over 30 brewpubs.

After a few semi-successful forays into the restaurant business, the McMenamins lobbied the Oregon legislature to change the laws which prohibited brewing and retail beer sales on the same premises. With added pressure from the Ponzis, founders of the Bridgeport Brewing Company, and others, the laws were finally changed and the McMenamin brothers opened the Barley Mill Pub on SE Hawthorne in Portland. The Hillsdale Brewery and Pub, also in Portland, followed in 1984 and began brewing in-house the following year.

McMenamins grew from these humble beginnings to the empire today by providing a clean, cozy and definitely funky atmosphere, a menu of quality pub fare, a commitment to employees and patrons (their slogan is "A Neighborhood Place for Family & Friends") and really good beer. Each brewpub has its own special features – from sit-down restaurants in strip malls, to remodeled houses, to taverns with pool tables – but all are recognizably McMenamins, owing largely to the psychedelic paintings on the walls, doors and even the restrooms. Three artists are staff employees of the company and have created a breathtaking array of coasters and signs for the various pubs, as well as recurring themes in the wall art.

In the mid-1980s, the company began to grow, adding such establishments as the Greenway Pub and the Blue Moon Tavern & Grill in Portland, the Riverwood Pub in Beaverton and the Lighthouse Brewpub in Lincoln City. In 1987, McMenamins opened several new pubs including the first combination brewpub/movie theater, the Mission Theater & Pub in Portland.

As establishments opened, the company developed a loose system of matching brewpubs with sister, non-brewing McMenamins taverns, each brewpub supplying beer to a different tavern. Some pairings are close in proximity, such as the Fulton Pub & Brewery which supplies the nearby Blue Moon; others are remarkably far from each other. For example, the Lighthouse Brewpub on Oregon's coast supplies beer to Mission Pub, while High Street Brewery & Cafe in Eugene supplies the Raleigh Hills Pub in Portland.

In 1990, the McMenamins began developing what would soon become a tourist destination in the microbrewing field and a veritable Disneyland for beer drinkers: Edgefield Manor in Troutdale, just up the Columbia River Gorge from Portland. This tremendous complex is a showcase for the famous McMenamins artwork – 14 artists spent an entire year painting every nook and cranny of the over 100-room lodge. Be sure to visit the amazing mural in the upstairs ballroom.

Another rapid growth year came in 1995, when McMenamins entered the Washington State marketplace and opened four brewpubs in just over six months. More McMenamins establishments are coming soon, including Dad Watson's in the Fremont district of Seattle, and The John Barleycorn Pub in Tigard, Oregon. The company is currently looking for a suitable place to open a theater/pub in Seattle. Two major new establishments of near-Edgefield proportions are in the works as well. The Crystal Ballroom, slated to open in downtown Portland, will offer three stories of excitement – a ground-floor billiards hall, a second-story brewery, and the restored ballroom on the third level, replete with jesters' heads on the beams, and featuring live music seven nights a week.

Further out on the horizon, the remodeled Kennedy School in NE Portland will open as a joint community redevelopment project between McMenamins and the city of Portland. This large space will contain the unlikely combination of brewery, bed and breakfast, community center/swimming pool, pub and police station. Where the McMenamins brothers will take us next, no one can say for certain. But it's sure to be fun...for the whole family.

McMenamins Beers

The Oregon Standards: Ruby Ale (a light ale brewed with a touch of raspberries), Terminator Stout, Black Rabbit Porter, Hammerhead, Cascade Head, Crystal (named for the Crystal Ballroom long before McMenamins acquired it), India Pale Ale

The Washington Standards: Ruby, Terminator, Crystal, Troll Porter, Temperance, Empire India Pale Ale

The Standard Seasonals:

Winter: Kris Kringle, Scotch
Spring: Raspberry Stout, Nebraska Bitter, Bock
Summer: Purple Haze, Strawberry Fields, Stella Blue (all brewed with berries)
Fall: Nutbrown

Other Favorites: Black Widow Stout, Maid Marion (brewed with marionberries), Hobbit's Habit (a very potent doppelbock), Rubinator (a popular mix of Ruby and Terminator)

McMenamins Establishments

East 19th Street Cafe
1485 E. 19th Street, Eugene, OR 97403
541/342-4025

High Street Brewery & Cafe
1243 High Street, Eugene, OR 97402
541/345-4905

McMenamins/Corvallis
420 NW 3rd, Corvallis, OR 97330
541/758-6044

Lighthouse Brewpub
4157 N. Hwy 101, Suite 117, Lincoln City, OR 97367
541/994-7238

Thompson Brewery & Pub
3575 Liberty Road. S., Salem, OR 97302
541/363-7286

McMenamins Brewery/West Linn
2090 SW 8th Avenue, West Linn, OR 97201
503/656-2970

McMenamins/Oregon City
102 9th Street, Oregon City, OR 97045
503/655-8032

McMenamins/Sunnyside
9751 SE Sunnyside Road #K, Clackamas, OR 97015
503/653-8011

McMenamins/Mall 205
9710 SE Washington Street, Suite A, Portland, OR 97216
503/254-5411

Highland Pub & Brewery
4225 SE 182nd, Gresham, OR 97030
503/665-3015

Edgefield Lodge/Brewery 503/669-8610

Black Rabbit Restaurant 503/492-3086

Power Station Pub 503/492-4686

Edgefield Winery & Tasting Room
2126 SW Halsey Street, Troutdale, OR 97060
503/665-2992

McMenamins/Sherwood
15976 SW Tualatin-Sherwood Road, Sherwood, OR 97140
503/625-3547

Fulton Pub & Brewery
0618 SW Nebraska, Portland, OR 97201
503/246-9530

Hillsdale Brewery & Pub
1505 SW Sunset Blvd., Portland, OR 97201
503/246-3938

Greenway Pub
12272 SW Scholls Ferry Road, Tigard, OR 97223
503/590-1865

John Barleycorns
14610 SW Sequoia Parkway, Tigard, OR 97223
503/684-2688

Riverwood Pub
8136 SW Hall Boulevard
Beaverton, OR 97008
503/643-7189

Raleigh Hills Pub
4495 SW Scholls Ferry Road, Portland, OR 97005
503/292-1723

McMenamins/Murray
6179 SW Murray Boulevard, Beaverton, OR 97005
503/644-4562

McMenamins/Cedar Hills
2927 SW Cedar Hills Boulevard, Beaverton, OR 97005
503/641-0151

Oak Hills Brewpub
14740 NW Cornell Road, Suite 80, Portland, OR 97229
503/645-0286

Cornelius Pass Roadhouse Brewery
4045 NW Cornelius Pass Road, Hillsboro, OR 97124
503/640-6174

Rock Creek Tavern
10000 Old Cornelius Pass Road, Hillsboro, OR 97124
503/645-3822

Bagdad Pub/Bagdad Theater & Pub
3702 SE Hawthorne Street, Portland, OR 97214
503/236-9234

Barley Mill Pub
1629 SE Hawthorne Street, Portland, OR 97214
503/231-1492

McMenamins on Broadway
1504 NE Broadway, Suite 900, Portland, OR 97232
503/288-9498

Market Street Pub
1511 SW 10th, Portland, OR 97201
503/497-0160

Mission Theater & Pub
1624 NW Glisan, Portland, OR 97209
503/223-4527

Blue Moon Tavern & Grill
432 NW 21st, Portland, OR 97209
503/223-3184

The Ram's Head
2282 NW Hoyt, Portland, OR 97210
503/221-0098

McMenamins Tavern
1716 NW 23rd, Portland, OR 97210
503/227-0929

John Barleycorns
14610 SW Sequoia Parkway, Tigard, OR 97223
503/684-2688

McMenamins on the Columbia
1801 SE Columbia River Drive, Vancouver, WA 98661
360/699-1521

Six Arms
300 E. Pike Street, Seattle, WA 98122
206/223-1698

McMenamins/Roy Street
200 Roy Street, Suite 105, Seattle, WA 98109
206/285-4722

McMenamins/Mill Creek
13300 Bothell-Everett Highway, Suite 304, Mill Creek, WA 98012
206/316-0520

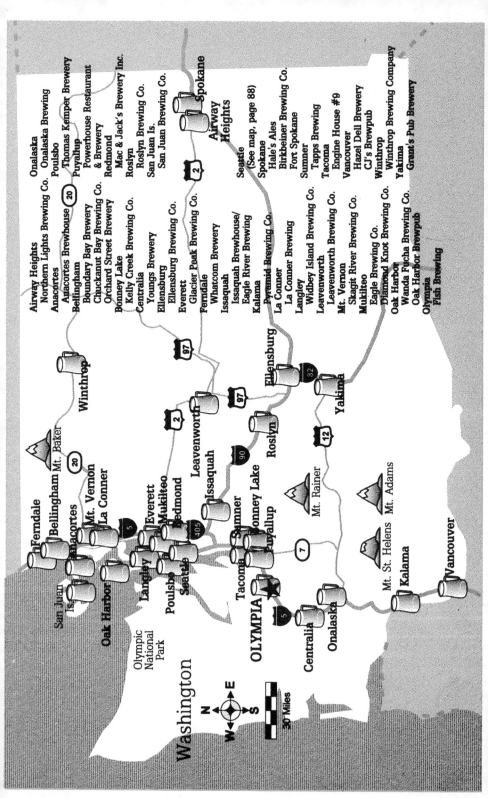

WASHINGTON

Washington is home to an incredible diversity of beers and brewers. From Redhook Ales, arguably one of the primary forces behind the resurgence of craft brewing, to small brewers like the Oak Harbor Brewery & Pub or Birkbeiner in Spokane, there is a beer and brewpub to satisfy every beer enthusiast.

The "alehouse," even more than the brewpub, is the site of critical beer tasting. In the Seattle area alone, dozens of alehouses, some with more than 30 beers on tap, offer a healthy selection of Washington's finest ales and lagers.

Seattle by no means monopolizes brewing in Washington, with only a dozen of the state's nearly 50 breweries located in the city. Wherever your destination in Washington, you can be guaranteed there is great beer close by!

CJ's Brewpub
11500 NE 76th Street A-B
Vancouver, WA 98662
360/253-5859

CJ's, located on the rural fringe of Vancouver, is one of the newest and smallest of Washington's brewing operations. Owner Connie Jean, aided by two homebrewers, uses a small three-barrel system to produce local craft brews for enthusiastic patrons.

CJ's is a casual spot for a simple meal and a pint of tasty ale. The restaurant is done in art deco style, with hand-painted murals covering the walls. Be sure to try CJ's specialties – half pound burgers, beer-battered fish and shrimp. Three standard ales are currently available. CJ's Nutbrown Ale is a mildly hopped, smooth, medium ale. CJ's India Pale Ale, a light amber ale with a mildly fruity finish, is the current pub favorite. The Amber Ale is also popular. Connie plans to brew a variety of seasonals as well as offering a series of homebrewing classes. The pub also pours several other regional brews, providing visitors with the chance to compare the styles and flavors of many Pacific Northwest beers.

Situated in a Safeway strip mall on the growing suburban edge of Vancouver, CJ's seems slightly out of place. The brewpub caters to a loyal, local clientele, however, who want to keep it right where it is.

Established: 1995

Hours: 11 am-10:30 pm Monday-Thursday, 11 am-11:30 pm Friday and Saturday, noon-9 pm Sunday

Children: Yes

Food: Burgers, sandwiches, salads

Entertainment: Pool, darts, television, juke box

Smoking: Yes

Payment: Visa/MC, Discover

Takeout: Yes

Directions: From I-205 in Washington, take Orchards exit, SR 500. At the fourth light, turn left on 76th. Street Brewery is in the Safeway shopping mall.

Hazel Dell Brewpub

8513 NE Highway 99
Vancouver, WA 98665
360/576-0996

The Hazel Dell Brewpub is a very unassuming place. Tucked between offices and a mobile home sales lot on Highway 99, it's easy to miss it if you're not looking closely. But once inside, with the noise and traffic of the highway left behind, you can get down to the wonderful work at hand – sampling various Hazel Dell ales.

The first thing you'll notice after entering the pub is the brewery, housed to the left of the bar. The elaborate larger-than-life hop vines painted in crawling and twisting designs on the heating and cooling ducts, the ceiling and the walls behind the bar will surely grab your attention next. The abundance of hops in Pacific Northwest beers, and the many hop farms that dot the landscape throughout the region are two of the primary reasons for the success of Pacific Northwest microbrewing.

Brewer Phil Stein produces several standard ales and four seasonals. Red Zone, a pale ale, is a highly hopped and fairly bitter brew, deep red in color. The name of the beer name refers to the area around Mt. St. Helens that was off limits after it erupted. Captain Moran's Irish Stout, a creamy and dense brew with coffee and chocolate flavors, is the brewery's darkest offering. Stein also produces the "Steinweizen," his own spin on a Hefeweizen. Hazel Dell's seasonal brews include an Octoberfest, Weihnacbier, a Winter Ale, a spring Steinbock and a summer Stoneberry, a golden ale flavored with marionberries.

Established: 1993

Hours: 11:30 am-11 pm daily, Friday until 1 am

Children: Yes

Food: Standard pub fare

Entertainment: Darts, regularly televised sporting events

Smoking: No

Payment: Visa/MC, Am Ex

Takeout: Yes

Directions: From I-5 south, take the 78th Street exit. At the bottom of exit, get in left lane and go left at the light onto Highway 99. The brewery is five blocks up on the right.

Pyramid Breweries, Inc.
110 West Marine Drive
Kalama, WA 98625
360/673-2121

Established: 1992

Hours: 10 am-4 pm Monday-Friday, also 10 am-4 pm Saturday in summer

Children: Yes

Food: No

Entertainment: No

Smoking: No

Payment: Checks

Takeout: Yes

Directions: From I-5 in Washington, take exit 27. At stop sign turn left. At first "T," go right. Go about 1½ miles along river. Brewery is on left.

Pyramid Breweries, Inc. (formerly Hart Brewing) was founded in 1984, making it one of the oldest Pacific Northwest craft brewing operations. The recently enlarged Kalama brewery on the Columbia River produces Hart's widely known Pyramid Ales. The brewery has also taken over brewing of the original Hart Espresso Stout, recently renamed Pyramid Espresso Stout. The new Hart brewery in Seattle mainly brews Thomas Kemper Lagers.

A tour of this massive facility – the brewery turns out about 90,000 barrels a year – is quite educational. Visitors are greeted by rows and rows of fermenters, while bottles blur past to be cleaned, filled, labeled and packed as the brewery rushes to keep up with demand. The tour ends at the tasting room, where many of the fine Pyramid Ales are on tap for sampling.

Pyramid Ales is in the process of adding a new "specialty" line of ales called the Pyramid Sphinx Series. Six draft ales will be offered around the Seattle area, with three; the Pyramid Porter, Kälsch (inspired by the German Kölsch, but with a little Kalama originality thrown in) and the winter Snow Cap Ale available throughout the Northwest. Beer enthusiasts can look forward to a rich and malty Scotch Ale on tap at the tasting room and around Seattle as part of the Sphinx Series as well.

Onalaska Brewing Company

248 Burchett Road
Onalaska, WA 98570
360/978-4253

The Onalaska Brewing Company, owned by Dave and Sue Moorehead, is a tale of home-brewing gone professional. The brewery is located behind Dave and Sue's rural home, surrounded by gardens, fields and forest. They use their own well water in the beer and enrich their soil and feed the local cows with the spent grains left over from brewing.

Onalaska Brewing produces three beers at present – Onalaska Ale, Red Dawg Ale and Howlin' Stout. Onalaska, the original brew, is a light, slightly fruity ale. Red Dawg Ale (not to be confused with Red Dog Ale, produced by Miller) is a darker, richer ale with a definite hoppy finish. Named for Cody, the Moorehead's Malamute dog who resides at the brewery, Red Dawg is especially good cask-conditioned and dry-hopped, with the extra hops and longer conditioning time bringing out the best in this beer. Howlin' Stout, the dark ale, is lighter than others on the market, appealing to those who want a heavier beer but don't want to use a spoon to drink it! Howlin' Stout uses just enough black malt to give it a slightly toasty, chocolate flavor.

Established: 1991

Hours: 8 am-5 pm Monday-Friday

Children: No

Food: No

Entertainment: No

Smoking: No

Payment: Checks

Takeout: Yes

Directions: Tours by appointment only. Please call for directions.

Youngs Brewing Company
5945 Prather Road SW
Centralia, WA 98531
360/736-7760

Youngs Brewing Company is the story of home-brewing getting out of hand and going crazily, desperately...right. Dick Young, owner and head brewer, added the brewery to his Northwest Sausage and Deli business in 1994. Visitors can sample any of the seven outstanding, hand-crafted ales as well as purchase the handmade sausages and smoked meats produced at the deli.

Dick was long famed in the local area for his homebrewing. The cry, "Dick's Beer is Here!" would often accompany Young when he entered a party with his cooler full of brew. The brewery now produces several standard ales in 22-ounce bottles, and the names are still familiar to the faithful-Dick's Wheaton, Dick's Cream Stout and the wonderfully dark and malty Dick Danger Ale. Dick's Harvest Ale, an Octoberfest-style ale, is also a must-try. Summer seasonal Raspberry Wheat is also worthy of a taste when available.

The brewery produced just over 150 barrels in 1995, making it one of the smallest operations in the Pacific Northwest. With growing distribution to Olympia, Tacoma and other cities, Young eventually hopes to boost production to over 500 barrels. For the moment, at least, "Dick's Beer" is one of the best kept secrets of the Pacific Northwest craft brewing renaissance.

Established: 1994

Hours: 9:30 am-5 pm Monday-Friday, 10 am-3 pm Saturday

Children: Yes

Food: Deli sandwiches

Entertainment: None

Smoking: No

Payment: Checks, Visa/MC

Takeout: Yes

Directions:
From I-5, take the Harrison Street exit. Go left at, go through all the lights and another three miles. Brewery is across the street from Cresent Grocers.

Fish Brewing Company

515 Jefferson Street SE
Olympia, WA 98501
360/943-6480

Established: 1993

Hours: 11 am-midnight
Monday-Saturday

Children: No

Food: Seafood appetizers,
salads, vegetarian and
meat & cheese sandwich-
es. The adjoining Levity
Cafe serves pasta and
wood-fired pizzas

Entertainment:
Acoustic musi-
cians play every
Saturday night

Smoking: No

Payment:
Checks

Takeout: Yes

Directions: From
I-5, take exit
105. Follow signs
for Port of Olympia onto
Plum Street. Take Plum
Street North about one
mile. Take a left onto 5th.
Brewery is on SW corner
of 5th and Jefferson.

Located in downtown Olympia, The Fish
Brewing Company is aptly decorated with a
charming variety of fish art – some owned by
the pub, but most for sale. A giant carved fish
mounted on the north wall watches over the
room. The brewery is visible through full-
length windows, with shining fermenters and
conditioners in plain view.

The smells of wood-fired
pizza from the adjoining
Levity Cafe and the rum-
ble of the occasional train
passing over the street in
front of the pub add to the
mellow feel of the Fish
Brewing Company. This
brewery is also deeply in-
volved in distribution, and
Fish Tale Ales are available
throughout Washington, in Portland, Oregon
and in taverns in the San Francisco East Bay
area.

The Fish Brewing Company offers a rotation of
six to eight regular and several seasonal ales
that always include at least one cask-conditioned ale. Pub favorite is the Fish Eye India
Pale Ale, a light, golden India Pale Ale that is
dry-hopped in the keg to add even more hops
to the finish. A strong second is the Fish's Best
Bitter, a traditional style English Bitter with a
lower alcohol content than other Fish Tale Ales.

Specialty and seasonal ales include the
Leviathan Barley Wine and Poseidon's Old
Scotch Ale, an ale brewed with peated malt,
which is used to make Scotch whiskey. The Fish
Brewing Company also offers an Octoberfish,
Winterfish Ale and Catfish Brown, which is
available during summer.

Engine House No. 9 Restaurant & Brewery

611 N. Pine Street
Tacoma, WA 98406
206/272-3435

Engine House No. 9 was built in 1907 and is the oldest surviving fire station in Tacoma. Besides the firehouse paraphernalia, the establishment now offers a distinct British pub ambiance, complete with darts, low ceilings and a step-up-to-order food counter. The bar (made in New Brunswick and originally part of the Old St. Louis Tavern in Tacoma) is situated in the back and is a superb example of woodcrafting. A favorite attraction of the locals is the 47-Beers-to-Taste Beer Club. Graduates who have tried them all earn a plaque which is displayed on the wall.

Between the Engine House and the brewery (located in a separate building) sits a true beer garden with tables scattered among trees. The food is quite tasty and the portions generous.

The Engine House and its sister establishment, The Powerhouse in Puyallup (see page 82), are fortunate to have brewer Adam Buff at the helm. Between the pair of seven-barrel breweries, Buff exercises his brewing creativity in two distinct brewing traditions. At the Engine House, he brews British-style ales; at the Powerhouse, German-style lagers. A visitor to either establishment enjoys the best of both worlds with beers from the other on tap along with the local brews. Appropriately, the Engine House serves its beers in 20-ounce imperial pint glasses.

Standard brews include Tacoma Brew, based on a recipe from Pacific Malting Company's pre-prohibition brewery in Tacoma; the aptly named Old Hop-Head; a light and refreshing Yorkshire Bitter; the Four Alarm Special Stout; a Scottish Ale; an Extra Special Bitter; and an India Pale Ale.

Established: 1995

Hours: 11 am-1 am Sunday-Thursday, 11 am-2 am Friday and Saturday

Children: No

Food: Pizzas, appetizers, sandwiches

Entertainment: Darts

Smoking: No

Payment: Checks, Visa/MC

Takeout: Yes

Directions: From I-5, take the Bremerton/Gig Harbor exit onto 16 West. Cross into the right lane quickly to catch the Sprague Street exit. Follow Sprague to 6th. Turn left on 6th, then right on Pine. The brewery is on the right.

Powerhouse Restaurant & Brewery

454 E. Main Street
Puyallup, WA 98372
206/845-1370

The Powerhouse Restaurant & Brewery is the sister establishment to Engine House No. 9 in Tacoma (see page 81). Both brewpubs are housed in turn-of-the-century brick buildings restored by the owner/architect, Dusty Trail, and both are on the historic registry. This building originally housed an electricity utility booster station, which explains the name and the recurring electrical theme in the décor.

The restaurant is a popular local eatery, with a menu that offers delicious options. Try the pizza with smoked salmon, capers and red onions in a dill sauce. The main dining room has a high ceiling, with an enormous philodendron hanging from the massive original wooden beams spanning the center of the building. Old electrical industry knickknacks adorn the walls. Stretching up one corner of the main dining room is a long electrical voltage carrier known as Jacob's Ladder, which sends an arcing current dancing up the wall any time a train passes by outside.

A small, square bar occupies the area immediately inside the front door, with the seven-barrel brewhouse visible behind a glass wall. This multi-level stainless brewery is set up in traditional gravity-fed vertical fashion, and is a striking sight from the dining area. The beers are Bavarian-style lagers, maerzens, bocks and pilsners made with all imported grains and hops. The standards include a Dunkel Weizen, an India Pale Ale, a Hefeweizen, the Four Alarm Stout, Powerhouse Porter and the delightful medium-bodied, German-style Amperage Alt, with plenty of smooth malt flavors and a fairly hefty body. In the winter, look for Old Knee-Knocker barley wine.

Established: 1995

Hours: 11 am-1 am daily

Children: No

Food: Pizzas, sandwiches, salads

Entertainment: Television, Jacob's Ladder

Smoking: No

Payment: Checks, Visa/MC

Takeout: Yes

Directions: From I-5, take 161 East or 167 East to Puyallup. On 161, follow it as it becomes Meridian about seven miles into Puyallup. Turn left on Main. The brewery is four blocks down on your left. On 167, follow it to 512 West. Then take the Pioneer Square exit. Turn left on Pioneer, then right on 5th. The brewery is in the three-story brick building.

Tapps Brewing

15625 Main Street
Sumner, WA 98390
206/863-8438

Tapps Brewing is a 20-barrel microbrewery brewing several lines of ales from a state-of-the-art brewhouse. Owner Doug Taylor renovated the building himself, after running a Boeing sub-contractor machine-shop in the same space for a number of years. He implemented his long-established practices of quality control and efficiency into his brewing. Tours are available by calling ahead, or you can enter the side of the building and stand in a foyer area to watch the brewing process.

The front of the building is a large tasting room with a patio out front. Locals bring food from McDonalds and Domino's pizzas into the plastic-and-formica seating area and wash it all down with Tapps beer.

The standard beers include Tapps Classic Ale, a good red ale with a nice balance between hops and caramel malts, a Winter Warmer Scotch Ale, a porter and a Weizen (malty, not yeasty). In the works are a Nutbrown, a stout, a berry ale, an Oktoberfest and cask-conditioned brews. The beers are bottled and distributed throughout 20 counties in Western Washington.

Established: 1995

Hours: 11 am-7 pm Monday-Thursday, 11 am-9 pm Friday and Saturday

Children: Yes

Food: No

Entertainment: No

Smoking: No

Payment: Visa/MC, Am Ex

Takeout: Yes

Directions: From I-5, take 161, 167 or 512 to 410 west. Follow 410 west to Sumner and exit onto Traffic Avenue. Follow Traffic to Main and turn right. Follow Main all the way through town to the 15,000 block. The brewery is on your left in the strip.

Kelley Creek Brewing Company

20123 Old Buckley Highway
Bonney Lake, WA 98390
206/862-5969

Established: 1993

Hours: Noon-8 pm
Wednesday-Sunday

Children: Yes

Food: No

Entertainment: No

Smoking: No

Payment: Checks

Takeout: Yes

Directions:
From I-5, take 161, 167 or 512 to 410 West. On 410 West, turn left onto the Old Buckley Highway just after the Bonney Lake entrance. Follow the Old Buckley Highway approximately 1½ miles through the countryside and watch for the brewery on your left, set back from the road behind a string of trees.

An idyllic farmland setting outside the sprawl of the Seattle area houses Kelley Creek Brewing. It is set up in a small, low-ceilinged dairy building, complete with all the original cement, stone work and accompanying out-buildings from 1928, the year it was constructed. The open fermenter sits in the main section of the dairy building, which doubles as the standing room-only tasting room. At the end of the day, locals often crowd in, bringing in their own containers to take beer home.

This countryside brewery is a great brew tour stop and is a refreshing change from the antiseptic style of most modern craft breweries. A make over complete with new equipment is in the works, financed by a public stock offering, so get there soon to experience this unique brewery setting. A good time to visit is late summer, when the company hosts mountain bike races on the premises. Kelley Creek also offer brewing classes – and you can take home the finished product.

The brewery specializes in ales with lots of honey and all whole-leaf hops. Their standards are Kelley Creek Honey Ale, a light amber ale; Silver Basin Honey Ale, a wheat ale with rounded malty flavor; and a Honey Porter. Past seasonals have included a Honey Rye Ale, a bock, a Märtzen-style Autumn Ale, Silver Basin Dark Honey Wheat, and various fruit beers, including a Black Cherry Ale. Kelley Creek beers are available throughout the Seattle, Kent and Tacoma areas at pubs and restaurants.

Redhook Brewery - Forecasters Brewpub

14300 NE 145th Street
Woodinville, WA 98072
206/483-3232

One of the Northwest's oldest microbreweries, Redhook poured its first beer in 1982. Owners Paul Shipman and Gordon Bowker have developed their Redhook ales into "cornerstone" brews of the Northwest and were instrumental in fostering Seattle's love affair with hops. Redhook's Ballard Bitter and its "Ya Sure Ya Betcha" slogan of quality (stated in Pacific Northwest Norwegian) are as familiar on area shelves as Budweiser.

The brewery continues to grow and has recently teamed up with Anheuser-Busch to take on the national market. The new bottling facility in Woodinville is the largest craft brewery in this area, with state-of-the-art equipment and nearly 100 conditioning tanks. The huge Krones bottling line alone is worth the $1 tour fee. Call ahead for tour times.

The 24-acre plot in the rolling foothills of Woodinville's wine country makes this is a picturesque stop. The pub is an enormous common area with long tables, plenty of natural light and high ceilings. The dark rafters on light plaster walls is reminiscent of Bavaria. The menu is short, offering basic pub fare. This is a destination public house. Expect a crowded seating area.

Established: 1994

Hours: Brewery: Call for tour times; Pub: 10am-10 pm Monday-Thursday, 10 am-midnight Friday, 11 am-midnight Saturday, noon-7 pm Sunday

Children: Yes, until 8 pm

Food: Standard pub fare

Entertainment: Live music Monday and Saturday

Smoking: No

Payment: Checks, Visa/MC

Takeout: Yes

Directions: From 405, turn West on 522. From 522, take the Woodinville exit onto 202 South. Follow 202 approximately three miles. The brewery is on the left, across the road from Chateau Ste. Michelle.

Issaquah Brewing Company

35 W. Sunset Way
Issaquah, WA 98027
206/557-1911

Established: 1995

Hours: 11:30 am-
11:30 pm daily

Children: Yes

Food: Pizzas, sandwiches,
burgers

Entertainment: Darts,
regularly televised sporting events, live
music

Smoking: No

Payment:
Checks,
Visa/MC

Takeout: Yes

Directions:
From I-90, take exit 17 to
Front Street. At the bot-
tom of the exit get in left
lane and go forward to
the second light. At the
light, turn right on to
Sunset. Brewery is on the
left.

Two doors down from the salmon hatchery is the recently opened Issaquah Brewing Company restaurant and pub. The owners originally intended the pub to be a small place with a focus on the distribution of draft ales. Luck and a bit of wisdom, however, changed all that, and the establishment has instead become a large pub and a restaurant. The result is a very attractive, comfortable space for family dinners, drinks with friends or a spirited game of darts. The specialty of the house is pizza – thick, chewy crust heaped with delicious cheeses and toppings.

The brewery, visible on the right side of the building as you walk in, is responsible for the five standards and two seasonals offered by Issaquah. Bullfrog, a wheat ale with lemon and lime juices added to produce a mild citrus flavor, is the most popular. Kodiak Jack Amber, Brass Rail Porter and Old's, a light ale with a dry crisp finish that comes from brewing with honey, are all available year round. Winter Haze, a delicious winter time favorite, and a summer Witbier are the current seasonals.

Twin Rivers Brewing Company/Sailfish Bar & Grill

104 N. Lewis Street
Monroe, WA 98272
360/794-4056

Established: 1995

Hours: Restaurant: 4 pm-midnight Tuesday-Saturday; Brewery: Tours by request

Children: Yes

Food: Fine dining

Entertainment: No

Smoking: No, in restaurant. Yes, in bar.

Payment: Checks, Visa/MC

Takeout: Yes

Directions:
From Highway 522, turn east on Highway 2. From Highway 2, turn south on Lewis Street and drive three blocks to Main Street. The restaurant is on the right, on the corner of Lewis and Main.

The Sailfish Bar & Grill was originally located in Seattle and moved to Monroe in 1993. Chef/owner Tim Kovach teamed up with his bartender, Steve Ladenhauf, and began producing small batches of beer for sale in the restaurant, brewing on the stove in the kitchen. The reception was overwhelming and now they have a four-barrel brewing system installed next door.

The restaurant is fairly upscale, with dark, wooden high-backed booths, an open kitchen and arching walls with old brick supports. The menu is impressive, offering such appetizers as roasted garlic custard, manilla clams and dungeness crab cakes. Traditional entrees include filet mignon and tiger prawns and a few exotic choices, such as the Thai stew.

Twin Rivers Brewing produces a collection of traditional-styled European ales and lagers, exploring all the great styles of German, English and Belgian brews, with recipes that are true to tradition, but often with their own twist. Some of the styles to date have included an India Pale Ale, a Saison Trappist with unmistakable flavors from the added coriander and orange peel, a hoppy and light-bodied English Brown Ale, an English Pale Ale, a rich and perfectly-hopped Imperial Stout and a German Alt. The company does not believe in brewing light beers, favoring brews with a high alcohol content. They are also beginning to keg their beer for draft markets in the greater Seattle area.

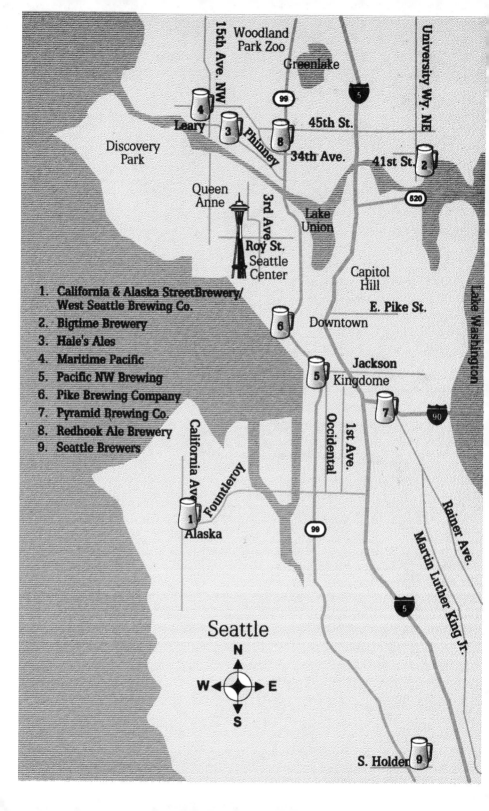

THE
SEATTLE
ALEHOUSE
EXPERIENCE

The growing demand for quality Northwest ales has led to the development of multi-tap pubs in almost every Seattle neighborhood. These alehouses, as they are called, offer 20 or more local and regional beers, providing a nearly inexhaustible selection to satisfy every taste.

Though certainly not unique to Seattle, the alehouse phenomenon has become the city's forté in the new craft beer age of the '90s. The alehouse setting is an ideal way for the casual beer enthusiast to sample beers from a variety of breweries in one sitting. You can taste-test multiple approaches to a given style, such as Hefeweizen, India Pale Ale or Porter, all in the relaxed atmosphere of a single alehouse.

Legend has it that the multi-tap alehouse phenomenon began in 1984, when Chris Barnes and Dan Cowen turned an average tavern into Cooper's Northwest Alehouse on Lake City Way. Their venture was a great success, and before long other entrepreneurs decided to tap into the alehouse concept. The success of these establishments is perhaps one reason why Seattle, compared to Portland or San Francisco, has few brewpubs. After all, given the choice between trying the ales of a single brewpub or sampling a wide variety of Northwest beers all at one establishment, many beer enthusiasts will opt for the latter.

With such tremendous exposure throughout the city, the breweries of Seattle thrive. And many have (or are planning) brewpubs. The Big Time Alehouse & Brewery in the University District is one of Seattle's oldest and most successful brewpubs. Pyramid Breweries, Inc. (formerly Hart Brewing Company), purveyors of Pyramid Ales and Thomas Kemper Lagers, recently opened a large pub on First Avenue near the Kingdome. Maritime Pacific Brewing Company on NW Leary Way will soon open a pub as well. But most brewpubs in Washington are outside the Seattle metropolitan area, serving smaller local populations.

There are numerous clusters of alehouses within the city, which presents several enjoyable tour possibilities. The collection of alehouses along 45th and University Avenue in the University District is an excellent example. Within a few blocks are such diverse public houses as The Blue Moon, The College Inn, Lox Stock & Bagel, The Unicorn and The Kerryman. The next step for the true enthusiast is a larger tour encompassing several of these clusters. Often Seattle neighborhoods blend into one another. Several more alehouses may lie just a few blocks away. Located at the famous Pike Place Market are both Kell's Irish Pub and The Virginia Inn (featured in the film "Singles"). While at the market, visit Pike Place Brewery for a tour and Liberty Malt Supply for homebrewing supplies.

A few blocks up First Avenue in Belltown is the Belltown Pub, known for its Brewmaster's Dinners, which match imaginative multiple courses with hand-crafted beers. Heading back down First Avenue is Pioneer Square's loosely-affiliated group of pubs, including The Bohemian, J&M's and the Pacific Alehouse. The Pioneer Square area is particularly good for pub crawls on weekend nights, when a single cover charge is good for entrance into all neighborhood pubs! However, this bargain often draws crowds of college students, resulting in long lines and plenty of waiting.

The following list of alehouses in the Seattle area, while definitely not exhaustive, will get you started. The alehouses are listed by neighborhoods, starting south and heading north up the I-5/Highway 99 corridor. Ask your favorite bartender for neighboring alehouses and breweries as well, and create your own mini-tour.

Alehouses of Seattle
Listed by Neighboring Districts

By no means a complete list, but sure to get you started.

Wedgwood

Wedgwood Alehouse & Café, 8515 35th Avenue NE, 206/527-2676
Fiddler's Inn, 9219 35th Avenue NE, 206/525-0826

Lake City Way

Cooper's Alehouse, 8065 Lake City Way NE, 206/522-2923

Maple Leaf

Reservoir Tavern, 8509 Roosevelt Way NE, 206/526-9737

University District

The Blue Moon, 740 NE 45th Street, Unlisted
The Kerryman Pub & Restaurant, 722 NE 45th Street, 206/545-2960
The College Inn Pub, 4006 University Way NE, 206/634-2307

Wallingford

Murphy's Pub, 1928 N. 45th Street, 206/634-2110
Pacific Inn Pub, 3501 Stone Way N, 206/547-2967

Ravenna

Duchess Tavern, 2827 NE 55th Street, 206/527-8606

Roosevelt District

Teddy's Tavern, 1012 NE 65th Street, 206/526-9174

Green Lake

The Latona By Green Lake, 6423 Latona Avenue NE, 206/525-2238
The Greenlake Alehouse, 7305 Aurora Avenue N, 206/781-8337

Phinney Ridge

74th Street Alehouse, 7401 Greenwood Avenue N, 206/784-2955
Woodland Park Pub, 6114 Phinney Avenue N, 206/784-3455

Fremont

The Dubliner, 3405 N Fremont Avenue, 206/548-1508
Red Door Alehouse, 3401 N Fremont Avenue, 206/547-7521

Greenwood

Cardiff Arms Alehouse, 9736 Greenwood Avenue N, Unlisted

Mad Dog Alehouse, 10200 Greenwood Avenue N, 206/782-9056

Ballard

The Backstage, 2208 NW Market Street, 206/789-1184

Ballard Firehouse Food & Beverage Company, 5429 Russell Avenue NW, 206/784-3516

Madison Park

The Attic Alehouse & Eatery, 4226 E. Madison Street, 206/323-3131

Queen Anne

Hilltop Alehouse, 2129 Queen Anne Avenue N, 206/285-3877

Belltown

The Belltown Pub, 2322 1st Avenue, 206/728-4311

Capital Hill

Comet Tavern, 922 E. Pike Street, 206/323-9853

Pike Place Market

Kell's Irish Pub, 1916 Post Alley, 206/728-1916

The Virginia Inn Tavern, 1937 1st Street, 206/728-1937

Pioneer Square

The Bohemian Café, 111 Yesler Way, 206/447-1514

J&M Café, 201 1st Street S, 206/624-1670

Alki

The Alki Tavern, 1321 Harbor Avenue SW, 206/932-9970

West Seattle

Westside Alehouse, 4421 Fauntleroy Way SW, 206/937-7607

Admiral Pub, 2306 California Avenue SW, 206/933-9500

Big Time Brewery
4133 University Way NE
Seattle, WA 98105
206/545-4509

Established: 1988

Hours: 11:30 am-12:30 am daily

Children: No

Food: Pub fare and deli sandwiches

Entertainment:
Shuffleboard

Smoking: Yes, in separate rooms

Payment:
Cash only

Takeout: Yes

Directions:
From I-5, take the 45th Avenue exit and turn east on 45th. Turn right on University, drive three blocks and the brewpub is on your right.

Big Time is one of Seattle's oldest brewpubs. Housed in an old tavern building with a handsome wooden bar dating back a century, the brewpub is decorated in traditional pub style, with beer artifacts adorning the walls. The brewhouse is visible through wall-sized windows behind the bar. This is not a particularly noisy place and does not offer loud music. Still, it's a bit too busy to curl up with a good book. The pub's most unique offering is the wall-mounted shuffleboard set in the back room. But be sure to sign up on the chalkboard to get a turn.

The deli sandwiches are hard to beat and are prepared behind a traditional deli-style counter. Layered with cold cuts and/or veggies stacked on various good breads, these sandwiches are the perfect complement to a fresh pint or two.

On any given day, the bar features six or seven beers on tap. These are sure to include Prime Time Pale Ale, Atlas Amber Ale and Coal Creek Porter. Other options are drawn from a pool of about 30 seasonals, such as Bhagwhan's Best India Pale Ale (unfiltered), Dublin Stout, Yulefest, Octoberfest, a Scottish ale, a Brown ale, an unfiltered rye, a barley wine, an Oatmeal stout, a pilsner and a couple of lagers. The most popular brew is Bhagwhan's Best India Pale Ale. Be sure to try the Northwest-style Amber. This beer has the hop kick without bitterness, sure to delight the hophead, and a nice depth of malt flavors.

Hale's Ales (Fremont)

4301 Leary Way
Seattle, WA 98107
206/782-0737

Established: 1995

Hours: 11 am-10 pm Monday-Thursday, 11 am-11 pm Friday-Saturday

Children: Yes, in a designated seating area, except on evenings with live music

Food: Upscale pub fare, salads, pizzas with spent-grain crust

Entertainment: Live jazz & blues on Wednesday and Saturday

Smoking: No

Payment: Visa/MC

Takeout: Yes

Directions: From I-5, take the 80th/85th Street exit. Take 85th west several blocks to 8th Avenue. Turn left on 8th and drive approximately three miles. Here 8th meets Leary Way at a diagonal, with only a left-turn as an option. Once on Leary, the brewpub is on your right, about a block down.

Hale's new Fremont brewpub is a neighborhood establishment showcasing this company's long tradition of quality brewing. The pub is decorated with rich colors and wooden trim. A striking oval bar, made of Honduran mahogany, defines the space lengthwise. The front area is furnished with comfortable sofas and chairs with a view from its large windows onto the street. The large back section houses the stage for live acoustic performances. The tantalizing menu offers appetizers like skewered tiger prawns, antipasto and a soft brewer's grain pretzel. The pizzas are gourmet, with toppings like grilled eggplant, spinach and black olive sauce.

The midsection of the pub looks out through a glass wall to the "arcade," an enclosed central area between the brewpub and the brewery, used for standing room on busy nights and the brewhouse beyond. It is an impressive new 30-barrel system and is most unusual in that its open-fermentation tanks do not even have covers, the froth of the fermentation process is visible on the rim of the lowest of the tanks.

Moss Bay Extra is an exceptional brew – the "extra" referring to the Northwest style of using huge amounts of malts and hops, lending great complexity. Some of Hale's other brews include O'Brien's Harvest, a Wee Heavy, an Irish ale, an India Pale Ale, a stout, and Tom Sheimo's Special Bitter named after Mike Hale's late partner. The pub has both beer engines and regular taps and rotates the different beers through both types of servers.

Pyramid Breweries, Inc.

91 S. Royal Brougham
Seattle, WA 98134
206/682-3377

Located just a few blocks from the Kingdome, Pyramid's (formerly known as Hart's) large new facility is housed in a brick building with massive wooden timbers. Built in 1913 for the Washington and Oregon Railway and Navigation Company, the structure now houses the brewery, a split-level pub and a retail store. Its center is dominated by a handsome refurbished copper mash tun manufactured in the 1940s, in Munich.

Inside, the pub has high ceilings and two balconies with additional seating. The whole interior has been rebuilt with handsome woodwork and is not warehouse-like as are many of the Northwest's brewpubs of comparable size. It is a popular and busy night spot – a good place to meet a whole group for the evening. The brewery proper is an equally spacious facility, with multiple conditioning and bright tanks, and a new bottling and kegging facility for both Thomas Kemper Lagers and Pyramid Ales.

Founded in 1984, Pyramid Breweries, Inc. encompasses two brewing ventures: Pyramid Breweries, Inc. of Kalama (see page 77) and Thomas Kemper Brewery of Poulsbo (see page 108). Because of this, brewmaster Randy Reed is able to offer an unusually diverse selection of beers. A few of the standard lagers available are a Munchener style Pale lager, a Dark lager, and an Amber lager. Pyramid's line of ales runs the gambit, from the old standbys of a hoppy Pale Ale and a rich well-balanced amber, to a Hefeweizen, a porter and their trademark Apricot Ale.

Established: 1995

Hours: Brewpub: 11 am-10 pm Sunday-Thursday, 11 am-11 pm Friday-Saturday; Brewery: Tours available

Children: Yes

Food: Upscale pub fare

Entertainment: No

Smoking: No

Payment: Checks, Visa/MC

Takeout: Yes

Directions: From I-5, take the Kingdome exit onto 4th. Turn right onto Royal Brougham and drive one block. The brewpub is on your left.

Maritime Pacific Brewing Company
1514 NW Leary Way
Seattle, WA 98107
206/782-6181

Established: 1990

Hours: Tours on the hour from 1 pm to 4 pm Saturday only

Children: Yes

Food: Bread made from spent grains from brewery

Entertainment: No

Smoking: No

Payment: Checks

Takeout: Yes

What was once an auto shop is now home to the Maritime Pacific Brewing Company. The brewery has recently increased production, and like the Puget Sound clipper ships of the seafaring past, Maritime Pacific is setting sail for new markets as it expands distribution. Growing from 3,000 barrels in 1994 to 6,000 in 1995 and adding a new bottling system help ensure that the brewery's well-deserved reputation will continue to spread. A brewpub, due to open soon, will provide a comfortable location for beer enthusiasts to sample this brewery's offerings.

Directions: From I-5 in Seattle, take the 45th Street exit. Travel West to 15th Avenue NW, turn left to the NW Leary Way exit. At end of exit turn right. Brewery is second building on right.

Maritime Pacific offers five standard ales, all brewed with wheat. Flagship Red Ale, the first beer brewed by the company, is the brewery's most popular ale. Red amber color, a slightly nutty flavor and a smooth finish make this an exceptional red ale. The four other standards are Clipper Gold Wheat Ale, a golden, light wheat ale; Islander Pale Ale; lightly hopped Nightwatch Ale; a smooth, dark amber; and Salmon Bay Bitter, a hoppy, bitter English ale. Seasonal ales include Bosun's Black Ale, Cape Lager and Jolly Roger Christmas Ale, an English-style Strong Ale with a high alcohol content (available November/December). Consistently of high quality, these and the five standard ales offer an impressive selection of unique flavors for the beer enthusiast.

Pacific Brewing Company Limited

322 Occidental Avenue South
Seattle, WA 98104
206/621-7002

Established: 1989

Hours: 4 pm-11 pm Wednesday-Friday, 11:30 am-2 am Saturday, 11:30 am-10 pm Sunday

Children: Yes

Food: Average pub fare with nightly dinner specials

Entertainment: No

Smoking: Yes

Payment: Visa/MC, Diners Club, Discover

Takeout: No

Directions: From I-5, take the Kingdome exit onto Royal Brauhm. Turn right onto First Street, then right onto Occidental. The brewpub is three blocks down and on your right.

Pacific Brewing Company Limited is one of Seattle's few true brewpubs. The warehouse-like interior has large windows facing one of the newest up-and-coming areas of Seattle – the old industrial district, just two blocks toward the water from the Kingdome. The pub's proximity to this sports arena makes this establishment a favorite stop both before and after games. If you're not a sports fan, go on a non-game day when you can enjoy the beer and the ambiance without the crowds.

The front of the pub is highlighted with an enormous, copper fermenting tank. Though just for show, it makes a handsome background to the wrap-around bar with its full liquor complement. Across from this bar is a side bar which faces a row of 10 attractive, wooden-cased serving tanks, each flowing directly to the bar. In nice weather, the ample sidewalk seating in front gives the place a nice urban feel.

There are five standard brews on tap and one seasonal. Offerings include a creamy Kölsch-style Blonde Ale; a Golden that's a bit lemony; a very interesting semi-sweet Amber Ale with a hoppy flare for a finish; a nicely balanced bitter; and a stout, which is strong, creamy and smoky. One of the seasonals is a Nutbrown, a dark and potent brew, strong and delivering that unmistakable nutty flavor.

THE PACIFIC NORTHWEST BREWING COMPANY, Ltd.

Pike Brewing Company

1432 Western Avenue
Seattle, WA 98101
206/622-3373

Established: 1989

Hours: 9am-5 pm
Monday-Friday

Children: No

Food: No

Entertainment: No

Smoking: No

Payment: Checks,
Visa/MC, Am Ex, Discover

Takeout: Yes

Directions: From I-5 in Seattle, take any downtown exit. Drive west to 1st Avenue. Brewery is located at 1432 Western Avenue, on the bottom level of the Pike Place Market. Liberty Malt Supply Company, the tasting room, is at 1419 1st Avenue, on the top level of the Market between Pike and Union.

Both the Pike Brewing Company and Liberty Malt Supply, located in the Pike Place Market, are home to a wealth of brewing information and experience. Liberty Malt Supply, Pike Place's tasting room, is also a home brewer's dream, with brewing equipment and ingredients in abundance. The brewery's beers have been written up internationally and have been described by beer critic Michael Jackson as some of the finest in the world.

Regular ales include Pike Place Pale Ale, XXXXX Stout, East India Pale Ale and Pike Place Porter. The Pale Ale, the brewery's most popular, is a slightly nutty, deep amber ale with a smooth finish. XXXXX Stout is a deep, chocolatey stout – one of the few that is also excellent from a bottle. Be sure to pick some up from Liberty Malt Supply. East India Pale Ale is a traditional India Pale Ale with a strong hoppy flavor and is often cask-conditioned.

In addition to the standards there are a number of specialty and seasonal ales. Auld Acquaintance, a spiced Christmas Ale, and Old Bawdy, a Barley Wine, are available in the winters. Cerveza Rosanna, made with three kinds of chilis; Birra Perfetto, spiced with oregano; and a garlic ale that is truly wonderful, add variety to the excellent traditional-styled ales brewed by Pike Brewing Company.

Redhook Ale Brewery-The Trolleyman Pub
3400 Phinney Avenue North
Seattle, WA 98103
206/548-8000

Founded in 1981, the Redhook Ale Brewery is one of the giants of the microbrewing revolution. Starting from a small neighborhood pub, the brewery is presently opening its third operation, this one in Portsmouth, New Hampshire.

The Trolleyman Pub, opened in 1988, is housed in the historic Fremont Car Barn, which served as the home of the Seattle Electric and Seattle Municipal railways at the turn of the century.

Redhook offers a number of standard and seasonal ales. The Redhook Extra Special Bitter, the most popular, is a smooth, consistent ale that is one of the best-selling microbrews in the region. Ballard Bitter, Blackhook Porter and Wheathook Ale are the other standards, all available in bottles and on tap at many bars and taverns. The brewery also produces a Winterhook, available fall and winter.

The current "Blueline" ale, the seasonal/specialty line, features the Redhook Rye; a brew with an unusual aroma, a rich, refreshing flavor and one of the very few rye beers presently on the market.

Established: 1981

Hours: 8:30 am-11 pm Monday-Thursday, 8:30 am to 12 am Friday, 11 am-12 pm Saturday, 12 pm to 7 pm Sunday. Call ahead for tour schedule

Children: No

Food: Pub fare and entrees

Entertainment: Bands play frequently

Smoking: No

Payment: Visa/MC, Am Ex

Takeout: Yes

Directions: From I-5, take the 45th Avenue exit west. Take 45th west to Fremont Ave (45th jogs into 46th at Aurora which is Hwy 99). Turn left on Fremont to 38th Avenue. Turn right on 38th to Phinney and turn left. Brewery is on the left.

Seattle Brewers

530 Holden Street
Seattle, WA 98108
206/762-7421

A banged-up building in the industrial section between Seattle and West Seattle houses Seattle Brewers. And, though this after-work joint is a bit out of the way and in a shabby area, it's an interesting place to stop. The brewery is in a distinct niche location, serving a local market, as breweries have always done.

Jerry's Jungle is the brewpub and depicts jungle scenery on the walls, along with beach scenes and knickknacks. The place has a distinct Jimmy Buffett feel, owing perhaps to owner and brewer Jerry Ceis' appreciation of the artist. The brewery is located behind the door marked "Gentlemen," which opens into the main warehouse part of the building. The brewhouse, keg storage and the men's room are located here.

Once the beer arrives at your table, you'll be glad you stopped at Seattle Brewers. At the top of the beer list is Alki Ale, an amber Scotch- style ale with nice, crisp malty flavors, a hint of hop and a fruity finish. It draws its name from the neighborhood and is the establishment's bestseller. Other beers include Bay Bitter, Puget Porter and a darned good Seattle Stout. If you're there on the right day, be sure to try the barley wine, Beaches Brew.

Established: 1992

Hours: 3:30 pm-7 pm Monday-Friday

Children: No

Food: No

Entertainment: No

Smoking: Yes

Payment: Cash only

Takeout: Yes, bring containers

Directions: From the section of Highway 99 south of downtown Seattle, take South Park/Holden Street exit. Head east toward the stoplight. (If coming from the north, go over 1st Avenue Bridge, stay in right lane, take the exit and cloverloop under the bridge.) At the stoplight, turn left on Holden. The brewery is in the second building on the left.

Seattle Brewing Company/ Aviator Ales

14316 NE 203rd Street
Woodinville, WA 98072
206/487-0717

This is one of the Seattle area's new and up-and-coming major microbreweries, and the sister company to the Willamette Valley Brewing Company, maker of Nor'Wester Ales. The Seattle Brewing Company is the producer of Aviator Ales, available in 12-ounce multi-packs and 22-ounce bottles throughout the greater Seattle area, as well as parts of Oregon and Alaska.

The company is in the process of developing a brewpub and restaurant in the rolling hills outside Woodinville. Its current facility is a straightforward brewery, located in a new, customized building at the edge of the suburban community of Woodinville. There is no tasting room, though there are regular tours and a shuttle bus for those coming from Seattle. Call for details.

After a four-year stint with Nor'Wester Ales in Portland, masterbrewer Brendan Smith moved back to his home state of Washington to head the operations at the Seattle Brewing Company. The brewhouse itself is a 50-barrel system with eight fermentation tanks, two bright tanks and a 130-bottle per minute bottling operation. The company kegs and bottles Aviator Ales, currently consisting of an amber, a Hefeweizen, a Honey Brown ale and a porter. Particularly tasty is the Amber, a refreshing brew with the right amount of hops in the aroma and a mellow body and finish. The first seasonal brew will be an India Pale Ale. The beers are all filtered, with the exception of the Hefeweizen.

Established: 1995

Hours: Tours by appointment

Children: No

Food: No

Entertainment: No

Smoking: No

Payment: N/A

Takeout: N/A

Directions: From Highway 522, take the 195th Street exit. Take 195th east to 144th. Turn left on 144th, go past the dead-end sign to the Do-Not-Enter sign. Turn left at the Aviator Ales sign.

West Seattle Brewing Company/ California & Alaska Street Brewery
4720 California Avenue SW
Seattle, WA 98116
206/938-2476

The West Seattle Brewing Company's California & Alaska Street Brewery is a local pub for local patrons. Battered couches, scuffed tables, an assortment of games, life-size Star Trek figures and yesterday's newspaper create a casual feeling – like you've just walked into a friend's family room for a beer. Only the large mash tun and brew kettle in the middle of the room give away that this is in fact a local brewery poised to expand into the regional market.

The brewery offers seven standard ales, a variety of seasonal and specialty ales and a root beer. A favorite of the locals is the Vashon Old Stock Ale, a golden, hoppy ale with a fruity taste. Admiral Extra Special Bitter, a fairly bitter amber ale, and Fauntleroy Stout, a smooth, dark ale, are also popular and when combined, they make Admiral Velvet, one of West Seattle Brewing Company's special blends. Special and seasonal ales include Top Hat Pepper, which is the Alki Ale aged in the keg with jalapeño and pepperoncini peppers, Pumpkin Ale, Raspberry Wheat, Three Grain Ale (barley, wheat and rye) and Umbock Alt. The pub also taps a fresh cask-conditioned ale every Friday night – which usually goes quickly!

Established: 1991

Hours: 3 pm-11 pm Tuesday-Thursday, 3 pm-12 am Friday, 12pm to 12 am Saturday, 4 pm-9 pm Sunday

Children: No

Food: Sandwiches, pizza bread, kosher sausage, garden burgers

Entertainment: Darts, board games, backgammon, occasional music

Smoking: No

Payment: Visa/MC

Takeout: Yes

Directions: Take I-5 in Seattle to the West Seattle Freeway. Go over the bridge to the top of the hill. At fourth traffic signal, take a right onto Alaska. Second signal is California. Brewery is 1/2 block to the left on the left side of street.

WASHINGTON'S "FOURTH CORNER"

The Northwestern corner of Washington is home to a remarkable cluster of breweries, well worth the voyage to this area known as "The Fourth Corner" of Washington, a site of stunning natural beauty, where the Cascade Mountains meet the sea.

The urban center of this area between Seattle and Vancouver, BC, is Bellingham – an eclectic city of 50,000, and home to three brewpubs, a "you-brew" facility, and one microbrewery. Start a brew tour at Boundary Bay Brewing Company, located next to the farmers' market at the edge of downtown. Don't leave without trying the outstanding Scotch ale.

Two of Bellingham's other breweries sit side by side on the north side of town. Chuckanut Bay Brewing, a brew-it-yourself facility, also offers bottled brews of its own to go. Next door is Orchard Street Brewery, where gourmet food compliments the many beers. Whatcom Brewery, the area's oldest brewing operation, does not offer scheduled tours, but look for Border Porter and Peace Arch Ale at area taverns.

One of the Northwest's most delightful brewery tours begins just south of Bellingham in the idyllic Skagit Valley. Visit the rustic Skagit River Brewing in Mount Vernon, the spiffy La Conner Brewing in La Conner, and the Anacortes Brewpub – home of an outstanding Belgian ale. A side trip from Anacortes to the San Juan

Islands and Friday Harbor's San Juan Brewing Company is also warranted, but deserves a day of its own.

From Anacortes, head South onto Whidbey Island, a wonderland of coves and isolated beaches, forest hikes and island villages. On your way, stop first at the Oak Harbor Pub & Brewery – on a nice day, relax outside on the patio. Then it's on to Coupeville and the Captain City Brewery, where an outstanding meal awaits you at the Front Street Cafe. End your island trek with a visit to the quaint village of Langley and a stop at the public tasting room of the Whidbey Island Brewing Company, where 10 hand-crafted beers await you.

A short ferry ride back to the mainland lands you in Mukilteo. Stop for a pizza or calzone dinner at Ripley's Pizza, home of Eagle Brewing, named after the area's first brewery, founded in 1870. Finally, finish the evening off with a game of pool at Cheers, Too, home to the beers of the Diamond Knot Brewing Company.

Glacier Peak Brewing Company

2929 Colby Avenue
Everett, WA 98201
206/258-1797, 800/718-2739

Glacier Peak is one of the new brewpub ventures in the Northwest made possible by a private stock offering. This is the first establishment, with more planned in the future. They are already doing a lively lunch business, catering to the downtown government workers with daily lunch specials. Evenings, this is a place for visiting with friends, over dinner or appetizers and a beer. It is a formulaic restaurant and brewery setting, with dark walls and wainscoting, a mug and bottle collection around the crown of the wainscoting and old photos of Everett and the Glacier Peak Wilderness Area. The fare is basic pub grub, such as potato skins, burgers and pizza.

An unusual feature is the ornately carved, cross-shaped bar area which houses twin staircases, one leading down to a yet unfinished lower level. Plans for downstairs include a homebrewers' library, a game room offering chess, backgammon and darts and a tasting room. Windows will look in on the lower half of the brewhouse. The other staircase leads up, to the handsome split-level brewhouse. This level is visible behind glass walls, designed to show off the shiny new 10-barrel system. A spiral staircase descends to the fermenters and the conditioning and bright tanks below.

Brews to date have included a Bitter for the ultimate hophead and a Winter ale which is also mighty hoppy. Planned future beers include the Monte Cristo Golden Extra Special Bitter, Wilderness Pale Ale, Milltown Brown and Home-Port Porter.

Established: 1996

Hours: 11 am-11 pm Monday-Thursday, 11 am-1 am Friday and Saturday, noon-9 pm Sunday

Children: Yes, until 9 pm

Food: Average pub fare

Entertainment: Live acoustic jazz and blues

Smoking: No

Payment: Visa/MC

Takeout: Yes

Directions: From I-5, take either City Center exit to Everett. Turn west toward downtown on either street and drive to Colby Avenue, the main street of town. Turn onto Colby toward the center of downtown. The brewpub is on the east side of the street, three doors south from the Everett Theater.

Diamond Knot Brewing Company/Cheers, Too

621 Front Street
Mukilteo, WA 98275
206/355-3446

Established: 1994

Hours: 11 am-2 am
Monday-Sunday

Children: No

Food: Quickie bar food

Entertainment: Pool and darts

Smoking: Yes

Payment: Checks

Takeout: Yes

Directions: From I-5, take the Mukilteo-Whidbey Island Ferry exit and proceed west on Highway 526. Follow the ferry landing signs to the off-ramp on the right. Pass this ramp proceeding straight down the hill to Front Street. The brewery and the bar are in the warehouse-like structure on your left.

Diamond Knot Brewing is a small brewery serving the Western Washington market of alehouses. It is situated in the coastal town of Mukilteo, the docking site for the ferry to Whidbey Island. Like its Mukilteo neighbor, Eagle Brewing (see page 107), Diamond Knot is simply a couple of brewers making quality beer on a small scale, and kegging it for distribution to retail outlets. The brewery is located in an old renovated bus barn, behind a smoky barfly's bar strewn with peanut shells. There are pool tables and darts to help you pass the time while awaiting the ferry, and the building provides shelter from the constant rain and mist.

The name Diamond Knot refers to a type of knot used by sailors. Specifically, however, it refers to a freighter ship that sank off the coast of Port Angeles in 1947. As the story goes, Farmers' Insurance Company almost went down with the ship due to the valuable cargo of canned salmon. A salvage operation, considered impossible, but attempted nonetheless, recovered the salmon. The insurance company was saved. Owner/brewers Brian Sollenberger and Bob Maphet liken the spirit of their small, but tenacious, brewing venture to the bulldog attitude of the insurance company determined to stay afloat.

Offerings include a truly authentic-tasting Hefeweizen, made with weinenstephan yeast. The most regular offerings are a porter and another especially authentic brew, the India Pale Ale. These beers live up to Diamond Knot's slogan: "Hand-crafted ales brewed locally – fresh and true to style."

Eagle Brewing Company/ Riley's Pizza

645 4th Street
Mukilteo, WA 98275
206/348-8088

One of the Pacific Northwest's reincarnated microbreweries is Eagle Brewing, named after an old, pre-prohibition local brewery. The original was built in 1870 by one of the European settlers of the area. The modern version is located in the basement of a converted house, with Riley's Pizza occupying the ground floor. Both are owned by Brian Sullivan, presently the mayor of Mukilteo.

Riley's Pizza is a family establishment in a homey setting with a gorgeous and very old wisteria vine and arbor over the front entrance. The main dining area and deck share a lovely view over Puget Sound and part of Mukilteo. Calzones are the house specialty, and the deep-crusted pizzas are also terrific.

Standard beers include Amber, Golden, Irish Red, Porter and Stout. Golden Eagle Ale, the most popular beer, is a very light amber with a full hop aroma and mild malts with a crisp finish. Cole's Porter is a rich, strong charcoaly drink named after Brian Sullivan's father, who was the general manager of the Butte Brewery in Montana. Brewer Bill Pearson has plans for a garlic beer for the next Arlington Garlic Festival, and later on, a lager.

Established: 1995

Hours: 11 am-9 pm Monday-Thursday, noon-10 pm Saturday, 4 pm-9 pm Sunday

Children: Yes

Food: Pizzas, calzones and sandwiches

Entertainment: Bands on special occasions, including St. Patrick's Day

Smoking: No

Payment: Checks, Visa/MC, Am Ex, Discover

Takeout: Yes, bring containers

Directions: From I-5, take the Mukilteo-Whidbey Island Ferry exit and proceed west on Highway 526. After entering the town, begin down the hill toward the ferry dock and turn right on 4th. The brewery and pizza parlor are one block up 4th on the right.

Eagle Brewing Company Riley's Pizza

Thomas Kemper Brewery

22381 Foss Road NE
Poulsbo, WA 98370
360/697-1446

Thomas Kemper is one of the Northwest's oldest and best-known microbreweries. It began in 1985 with two environmental engineers brewing small batches of premium lagers. Demand for the tasty, locally-brewed beer drove them to a bigger location on the Kitsap Peninsula the very next year. In 1992, Hart Brewing (now Pyramid Breweries, Inc.) purchased Thomas Kemper Lagers, and the sky's been the limit ever since.

Despite booming sales, the Poulsbo taproom has not changed much since its beginnings. It's still a sleepy, country tavern set amidst meadows and stands of conifers, with just a few picnic tables, a 1970s model TV tucked away on a shelf full of beer knickknacks, and a make-shift kitchen. The brewhouse itself is equally funky. In the near future, though, Pyramid Breweries' new facility in Seattle will take over the production of Kemper draft lagers, and the ramshackle barn in Poulsbo will become a testing-ground for new beers.

The brewery features several beers, as well as few of Kemper's increasingly popular sodas. Always available are the Northwest-style Hefeweizen, the ale-like Amber, the Helles Blueberry, the Pale Lager (the only lager they don't bottle) and the Weizen Berry. Seasonally, look for Rollingbay Bock, Oktoberfest, a Bavarian Dunkel-style Dark lager, a filtered Honey Weizen, and the only ale, a deliciously light and crisp Bavarian Wit, boiled with chamomile instead of hops. Sodas include honey vanilla cream soda, birch soda and root beer.

Established: 1986

Hours: 11 am-8 pm Monday-Thursday, 11 am-10 pm Friday and Saturday, 11 am-6 pm Sunday

Children: Yes

Food: Limited menu of burgers, sandwiches and nachos

Entertainment: Occasional live music

Smoking: No

Payment: Checks, Visa/MC

Takeout: Yes

Directions: From the Kingston ferry dock, drive straight south eight miles to the Thomas Kemper sign on the right. Turn right and drive 1/4 mile, the brewery is on your left. From Bremerton by Highway 3, drive to Poulsbo junction. Turn northeast toward Kingston and drive about two miles. Turn left at the Kemper sign. From Bainbridge Island, follow Highway 305 through Poulsbo to the Poulsbo junction and turn northeast.

Whidbey Island Brewing Company

630-B Second Street
Langley, WA 98260
206/221-8373

Established: 1992

Hours: Noon-6 pm
Monday -Thursday, noon-
8 pm Friday, noon-6 pm
Saturday, noon-5 pm
Sunday

Children: Yes

Food: No

Entertainment: No

Smoking: No

Payment: Checks

Takeout: Yes

Whidbey Island Brewing Company is situated atop the hill overlooking the quaint New England-style town of Langley and the leg of seawater between the island and mainland. It is a small, brightly-lit tasting room with four picnic tables and 10 beers on tap. Note the outstanding collection of antique beer trays on the wall.

What began as a 10-gallon brewery has grown to a 10-barrel brewing operation, and now serves as the base for one satellite brewpub in Oak Harbor (see page 111) and others to come. Much of the brewery's original equipment (including a homemade grain mill) was built on the island by local tradesman. Beers are available in bottles and on draft in taverns throughout Western Washington.

Self-trained brewmaster and proprietor, Jim Grimes, favors German-style low-hop, maltier recipes. The hallmark offering is Whidbey Ale, a light amber, smooth ale, with the perfect touch of hops. Their Langley Light Ale is a good thirst quencher, with more complex flavor than your average light. If you like berry beers, they've got a great one in Bayview Blackberry Ale. The hoppiest beer is Cascade Pale Ale, light but very aromatic. They also brew root beer for kids of all ages.

Directions: Drive straight off the ferry just over a mile to Highway 525, to sign "Langley next right." Turn right and drive 1½ miles; take another right and drive to T in road. Turn left, drive into town, turn left on Second Street and go to the crest of the hill. The brewery is on your right. From Northern Whidbey Island, follow Highway 525 toward the Mukilteo ferry dock until you see the sign for the Langley turnoff on the left. Take it and drive to the T mentioned above and proceed into town.

Captain City Brewery/ Front Street Cafe

23 Front Street
Coupeville, WA
360/678-9080

Named for Coupeville's original nickname, the City of Captains, Captain City Brewing is Whidbey Island's third brewery. Mariner's Court Building, overlooking the water at the edge of this charming little town, houses the brewery. While it's tucked in the back of the building, it's visible from the side street and the entrance corridor.

Also housed in this weatherbeaten structure are Christopher's, a restaurant of some sophistication, and the new spinoff front section called the Bay Front Cafe, which serves as a more casual eatery and as a small taproom for the brewery. The cafe's food is mouthwatering, and the view looking out over the pier is perfect. The menu includes salads, gourmet sandwiches, local seafood and several entrees. The Cajun seafood crepe is truly outstanding. The more formal Christopher's offers a full selection, with appetizers such as escargot and Greek salad, and entrees featuring Thai prawns, salmon baked in filo and pork loin medallions in a blackberry-almond sauce.

Captain City's owner/brewer Kevin Locke comes from Napa Valley Brewing Company via the first class of the American Brewer's Guild Apprenticeship Program taught by Michael Lewis. Locke likes to brew hoppy beers including Coupe's Success Cream Ale, Barry Burton's Roof Top Red, and local favorite, Skookum Stout. In the works are Parrothead Amber, a contract brew for Toby's Tavern down the street, and Blockhouse barley wine. Locke also offers homebrewing classes on the premises.

Established: 1996

Hours: Brewery: 9am-5 pm Wednesday-Sunday (call ahead for tours); Restaurants: 11 am-9 pm Monday-Sunday

Children: Yes

Food: Casual and fine-dining

Entertainment: Baby grand piano, live jazz and blues

Smoking: No

Payment: Checks

Takeout: Yes

Directions: From Highway 20, turn east toward Coupeville City Center at the light by the pedestrian overwalk. This becomes Main Street. Follow Main Street all the way to the water and turn left on Front Street. The brewery and restaurant are in the gray building on the left at the far end of Front Street.

Oak Harbor Pub & Brewery

6405 NW 60th Avenue
Oak Harbor, WA
360/675-7408

Established: 1996

Hours: 11 am-11 pm
Monday-Thursday, 11 am-
1 am Friday and Saturday,
11 am-11 pm Sunday

Children: Yes, in certain
areas

Food: Full menu

Oak Harbor Pub is one of the new multiple-environment brewpubs with something for everyone. Located in the heart of the town, it's an ideal stop for island explorers. The facility is divided into diverse spaces that include a restaurant area and lunch/pub counter with a live music stage, a fenced-in patio, a pub room with sports on the TV, jukebox and dart lanes, a snug area with cozy furniture around a stove and a gameroom set in back with pool tables and pinball machines.

Entertainment:
Live music,
pool, darts,
pinball,
television

Smoking:
No

The menu, ideal for lunch or a light dinner, includes pastas, steaks, seafood and sandwiches with a specialty assortment of sausage sandwiches.

Payment:
Checks, Visa/MC,
Discover

Takeout: Yes

The brewhouse is small and tucked in a windowed room by the front entrance to the restaurant. All of the brews are available on the 28 taps in the brewpub. Selections include Whidbey Ale, Island Stout, Cascade Pale Ale, Bayview Blackberry and Langley Light. Brewer Kelly Taylor, formerly of Diamond Knot and Eagle Brewing, has created a few new brews as well. Oak Harbor Dutch Style Ale features a Belgian yeast and the addition of rock candy. Soon to come are Kelly's Irish Ale, an Oatmeal stout and an India Pale Ale.

Directions: From I-5, take Highway 20 to Oak Harbor. The brewery is on the west side of the street, just north of 70th Avenue West.

Anacortes Brewhouse

320 Commercial Avenue
Anacortes, WA 98221
360/293-2444

The Anacortes Brewhouse is a restaurant-pub, with a laid-back atmosphere. The building itself dates from 1929, when it was Bogart's Saloon. Note the impressive original bar, built of mahogany, poplar and birch.

Anacortes is a quaint setting for a brewhouse, serving as the port of call for the primary San Juan Island ferry runs and adorned with a handsome series of antique-style murals throughout the downtown area. The art theme continues inside the brewhouse, where work of the establishment's artist in residence, Dick Garvey, decorates the walls.

The menu is a mix of traditional pub fare and daily specials, showcasing the region's fine seafood. They're doing wood-fired pizzas and doing them well – try the pesto!

Brewer Paul Wasik brews some excellent, traditionally-styled beers. Standard offerings are Longboat Lager, an aged pilsner with that unmistakable Saaz aroma and crisp lager finish; Flashing Amber Ale, a full-bodied Northwest-style Amber; River Otter Porter, a chocolatey porter; and a Scottish ale that's hoppier than your average Scottish, but balanced out with the complexity of six malts and the usual Scottish kick. Past seasonals have included a Maibock, a Rye Ale, Searun Stout, White King Hefeweizen, Old Pal barley wine, a Noel Lager and a Lagered Cream Ale. The Belgian is outstanding and the Dopplebock is concentrated and very tasty.

Established: 1994

Hours: 11:30 am-9 pm Sunday-Thursday for dinner, pub open later; 11:30 am-10:00 pm Friday and Saturday for dinner, pub open later

Children: No

Food: Pub fare, exotic pastas, wood-fired pizzas

Entertainment: Board games/backgammon, darts, live jazz first Sunday of each month

Smoking: No

Payment: Checks, Visa/MC, Am Ex, Discover

Takeout: Yes

Directions: From I-5, take Highway 20 west 17 miles. Highway 20 becomes Commercial Avenue as it enters Anacortes. Continue north on Commercial through town to the corner of 4th and Commercial. The brewhouse is on your left.

San Juan Brewing Company – Front Street Ale House

One Front Street
Friday Harbor, WA 98250
360/378-2337

Established: 1993

Hours: 8 am-midnight Sunday-Thursday. 8 am-1 am Friday and Saturday

Children: Yes, in the restaurant

Food: Traditional English and American pub fare. Open breakfast, lunch and dinner. Children's menu available

Entertainment: Steel tip darts, sports on TV, acoustic musicians

Smoking: No

Payment: Visa/MC

Takeout: Yes

When docking at Friday Harbor on San Juan Island, one of the first establishments you'll notice in this summer resort town is the Front Street Ale House, home of the San Juan Brewing Company.

From the inside, views of the water and surrounding islands make for a scenic place to sip the only local suds on the islands. The cheery atmosphere has a neighborhood feel, and, yes, between the tourists, you'll find faithful locals.

The brewery produces about 30 different beers each year, approximately a quarter of them first-timers. The crowd favorite, and the only one brewed continuously, is the Eichenberger Hefeweizen. Also popular is the winter brew, Raging Main Ale, known for its high octane kick. For something off-beat, look for one of the laced beers, such as No Vamp Ale, flavored with elephant garlic and served around Halloween; Hot Harry's Pepper Beer, seasoned with jalapeño; or Java Ale, a coffee-infused Brown ale.

In addition to beer, the pub offers a huge 16-page menu covering everything from French toast to Bangers and Mash. The predominantly English and American fare is available for breakfast, lunch or dinner.

Directions: Take the ferry from Anacortes to Friday Harbor. The pub and brewery are located on the corner of Main and Front streets and are visible from the ferry landing.

La Conner Brewing

117 S. First Street
La Conner, WA 98257
360/466-1415

Established: 1995

Hours: 11:30 am-10 pm
Sunday-Thursday, 11:30
am-11 pm Friday and
Saturday

Children: Yes

Food: Wood-fired
gourmet pizzas, salads,
appetizers

Entertainment: Television
at the bar

Smoking: No

Payment:
Visa/MC

Takeout: Yes

Directions:

The La Conner brewpub is housed in a new structure at the edge of town near the water. The outside of the building is striking and handsome, and the interior is small and upscale. The magnificent light pine columns and facades and the open kitchen with its wood-fired oven give the brewpub a comfortable feel. In nice weather, there is outdoor seating.

The menu focuses on pizzas and offers a variety of toppings, from feta and calamatas to smoked salmon, roasted chicken and spinach.

The 10-barrel brewery is in the same building as the pub but is not visible. The beers are all served in traditional European glassware, including schooners, British pints and many others. Standard offerings include a light, creamy pilsner; a smooth and smoky stout; a Brown ale that is fairly light-bodied, but nicely balanced between sweet and dry; a refreshing wheat; and a root beer. Other seasonal brews include an India Pale Ale, a Spring bock, and for the winter holidays, Tannenbaum Ale, a spicy and nutty British-style ale.

The town of La Conner is an historic centerpiece to this area. With its handsome houses and antique shops, it feels like a Western town caught sometime in the early part of the twentieth century. The Skagit Valley Tulip Festival, held annually in the spring, is a major tourist attraction to the area.

From I-5, take exit 221 and head west. Take the first quick right. Go through Conway and cross the Skagit River onto Fir Island Road. Proceed as it becomes Best Road, then turn left onto Chilberg Road. Go to stop sign and turn left on La Conner/Whitney Road, which becomes Morris Avenue as it heads into La Conner. Follow Morris to the end of town and turn left on First Street. The brewpub is on the left

Skagit River Brewing Company
404 Third Street
Mount Vernon, WA 98273
360/336-2884

Established: 1994

Hours: 11 am-8 pm Monday-Thursday, 11 am-11 pm Friday and Saturday, 11 am-6 pm Sunday

Children: Yes

Food: Soups and sandwiches

Entertainment: Live acoustic and full band music, swing dance classes

Smoking: No

Payment: Checks, Visa/MC, Am Ex

Takeout: Yes

Directions: From I-5, take the Mount Vernon City Center exit and turn west on Kincaid. Turn right on 3rd and drive two blocks. The brewery is on the right.

This is a microbrewery with a large taproom that feels like a brewpub. Skagit River Brewing is housed in what was once home to the Pacific Fruit & Produce Company. This handsome, 1928 brick building sits near the railroad tracks at the edge of downtown and is a nice place to gather, both inside or outside, on the roofed back porch. For a romping time, dance to live music on the hardwood floor. Art that changes with the seasons lends a warm atmosphere to the main seating area. Stairs lead up to a more intimate balcony area.

Skagit River downplays the taproom, concentrating instead on expanding the draft market from the Canadian border down to Pierce County. The brewhouse, visible through a glass wall at the back of the taproom, is a 10-barrel system. To help keep up with demand for Skagit River brews, additional fermenters and conditioning tanks will soon be on line.

Brewer Charlie Sullivan, who worked at McMenamins for three years prior to opening Skagit River, brews several standard ales including a lager-like Dutch Gold, flavorful without the full-on hops of a traditional lager; an English-style Nutbrown called Steelie Brown, brewed with a touch of oats in the mix; and Highwater Porter, a light-bodied porter with plenty of hops. Other brews include a very smooth, roasty and strong Russian Imperial Stout, Blackhorn Bock Lager and a contract brew available only at the Snoqualmie Pass Ski Area that is 50% rye, light and very quaffable.

STEELIE-BROWN

SKAGIT RIVER BREWING COMPANY
ALE
(360)336-2884

Boundary Bay Brewery and Bistro

1107 Railroad Avenue
Bellingham, WA
360/647-5593

Named for the next bay north from Bellingham Bay, this brewery is a gem. Boundary Bay is a hometown pub and eatery in a refurbished warehouse space at the edge of downtown. The interior is divided into the taproom; the pub-like area with many tables and a bar; and the bistro, a large high-ceilinged room with the sconce-like lighting, old bricks and wood lending it a medieval flavor. The handsome tables and bar are made from salvaged flooring and are combined with an admirable collection of antique, mismatched chairs. The taproom also has a large garage door that leads to the sidewalk. In warm weather, the owners open the door to bring in the fresh air. The menu offers a mix of hearty stews, European-style meat and potatoes and lighter options such as pastas, salads, and seafood.

The brewhouse is a glassed-in room beginning in the corner of the taproom and stretching the length of the building, with additional facilities in the basement. Ed Newman, owner and head brewer, makes excellent, unfiltered beer. A tremendous Scotch ale, thoroughly malted with lots of fruit esters, is very tasty. The amber is an excellent example of a fully hopped amber that isn't astringent, and the porter is deep ruby-brown with the right combination of roasted and mellower malts. The first two seasonals, a holiday ale and an Oatmeal stout, were quite impressive.

April to October, the local farmer's market operates right in front of the brewery. A scenic walking/cycling path also passes by the brewery, through the length of Bellingham and down the coast to Chuckanut Bay and beyond.

Established: 1995

Hours: 11 am-11 pm Monday-Wednesday, 11 am-midnight Thursday-Saturday, 3 pm-10 pm Sunday

Children: Yes, in the Bistro

Food: Full lunch and dinner menu

Entertainment: Television for special events, regular bands and live acoustic music

Smoking: No

Payment: Checks, Visa/MC, Discover

Takeout: Yes

Directions: From I-5, take the Lakeway Drive exit in the heart of Bellingham. The ramp merges right onto King. In a block, turn right on Lakeway Drive, pass under the highway to a five-way intersection. Veer right onto Holly and drive five blocks into town to Railroad Avenue. Turn left on Railroad and the brewery is on your right at the end of the street.

Chuckanut Bay Brewing Company

709 W. Orchard Drive, Suite 5
Bellingham, WA 98225
360/734-4223

Established: 1995

Hours: Winter: 11 am-6 pm Monday-Saturday; Summer: 11 am-8 pm Monday-Saturday

Children: Yes

Food: No

Entertainment: No

Smoking: No

Payment: Checks, Visa/MC

Takeout: Yes

Chuckanut Bay is an interesting hybrid. One of Washington's few "you-brew" establishments, the brewery also produces and bottles four beers for sale in retail outlets throughout the area. Or, sample and purchase them at the brewery.

The copper brewhouse sits in the front windows of the long, narrow space. A row of shiny, new mini-fermenters, available for customer use, sits along one wall. Folks come in, pick out their favorite beer, and go through the process of actually making it, under close supervision. There is a fee for the instruction, ingredients and bottles. Everything else – from the recipe, to the brewing setup, to the filter at the end of the process – is provided.

The brewery's own beer line includes three ales and a crisp, golden pilsner. All ales are classic Northwest-style brews, including a creamy and smooth Red ale, a Wheat ale, and a rich, chocolatey porter. This is the only line of bottled beers currently produced in Bellingham.

Directions: From I-5, take the Meridian Street exit and turn south toward the city center on Meridian. Drive about two blocks and turn left on Orchard Street. Go about three blocks to West Orchard Drive. Turn right and enter the parking lot on your right. The brewery is to the left of the middle of the long building.

Chuckanut Bay is a fun addition to the brewing scene in Bellingham. For tourists passing through, it makes a great stop for a few bottled beers to go, as well as an introduction to the interesting world of "you-brews" (see page 177). For those in the area, it is an invaluable resource as the only homebrew supply store in Bellingham, and serves the growing population of folks who want to try brewing without the expense of doing it at home.

Orchard Street Brewery

709 W. Orchard Drive, Suite 1
Bellingham, WA 98225
360/647-1614

Orchard Street is a medium-sized micro-brewery located in a semi-industrial area just off Bellingham's main commercial strip. An upscale restaurant occupies the front of the building and is an intimate place where folks stop on the way to work for a pastry, meet for a business lunch or gather at the end of the day for a nice dinner and good beer.

The menu offers several appetizers, including baked brie and marinated tiger prawn salad. Entrees feature salmon en crute and madeira glazed filet mignon. The specialty, however, is wood-fired pizza. Try the seafood, feta and tomato pizza pie! The 20-barrel brewhouse with combination mash/lauter tun and kettle/whirlpool are visible behind the rear glass wall of the bar area, adding to the restaurant's charm.

Owner/brewer Christian Krogstad comes from a long tenure at McMenamins where he managed several of the establishments including Edgefield (see page 58). He makes an assortment of unfiltered beers true-to-style with a variety of yeast strains. The current standard lineup includes a fairly clear Hefeweizen, an excellent complex and malty Stock Ale made to enjoy with food, a Northwest-style Pale Ale flavored with Cascade hops flowers for a not-too-sweet finish, and Christina Porter with lots of chocolate malt flavor. Recent seasonals include a Kölsch-style Golden ale with 20% wheat in the mix, and Jingle Ale, a strong, spicy winter brew. Orchard Street kegs its beer for distribution throughout the Puget Sound area.

Established: 1995

Hours: Restaurant: 7 am-10 pm Sunday-Thursday, 11 am-10 pm Friday-Saturday; Brewery: Tours on demand or call for brewery tour times

Children: Yes

Food: Casual and fine dining

Entertainment: No

Smoking: No

Payment: Checks, Visa/MC, Am Ex

Takeout: Yes

Directions: From I-5, take the Meridian Street exit and turn south toward the city center on Meridian. Go two blocks and turn left on Orchard Street. Follow Orchard about three blocks to West Orchard Drive. Turn right and enter the parking lot on your right. The brewery and restaurant are at the right end of the long building.

Whatcom Brewery

P.O. Box 427
Ferndale, WA 98248
360/380-6969

The Whatcom Brewery produces ales from a truly land-based, bio-regional perspective. Owner Lloyd Zimmerman and brewer John Hudson are working with a local hops grower to produce the only strain of Czeck Saaz hops in Western Washington. They trade spent grains to a pig farmer in return for pigs. And they have cobbled together one of the most original brewhouses (using, as they put it, 97% recycled materials) in the Northwest. It is completely gravity fed, from the mill tucked away under the rafters, to the open fermenter on the ground floor of this turn-of-the-century-pioneer-cabin.

Zimmerman and Hudson are in the process of turning the top floor of the building into an elaborate brewer's quarters, complete with sliding bookcase and totem-style wood carvings. They plan to turn the place into a brewing institute, with accommodations for a brewing apprentice to live and work in the brewery for a week of intensive study.

Whatcom Brewery offers two standard ales – Peace Arch Pale Ale, named for the arch at the border crossing a few miles north of Ferndale, and Border Porter, a rich, chocolatey brew. The two planned seasonal brews are Chuckanut Brown Ale for the spring and Baker Bitter for the fall. For the winter holidays, a touch of cinnamon is added to the porter. This is a drink well worth seeking out. The beers are primarily available at regional establishments in Whatcom County, but have been sighted on tap in Seattle and Mount Vernon. Look for Zimmerman's hand-carved tap handles.

Established: 1994

Hours: Tours by appointment

Children: No

Food: No

Entertainment: No

Smoking: No

Payment: N/A

Takeout: No

Directions: Call for directions

Roslyn Brewing Company

208 Pennsylvania Avenue
Roslyn, WA 98941
509/649-2232

Established: 1990

Hours: Noon-5 pm
Saturday and Sunday
(Noon-6 pm in the summer)

Children: Yes

Food: None

Entertainment: Acoustic
musicians play occasionally

Smoking: No

Payment: Checks,
Visa/MC

Takeout: Yes

Directions: From I-90,
take exit 80. Follow signs
to Roslyn (three miles).
Turn left at Pennsylvania
Avenue. Brewery is 1½
blocks down on left.

The Roslyn Brewing Company, located in the quiet town made famous as the filming location for the "Northern Exposure" TV series, is an historically rooted brewery. The Roslyn Brewing and Malting Company, founded in 1889, brewed beer for the locals working in the booming coal mines until Prohibition closed it in 1913. Brewers Roger Beardsley and Dino Enrico opened the Roslyn Brewing Company in 1990 to rekindle the tastes, styles, and traditions of the former brewery.

Beardsley and Enrico brew two beers, both lagers – a rarity among modern craft breweries. Roslyn Beer is a smooth, dark lager. Brookside Beer is a light, pale lager. The longer and colder conditioning of these lagers produces beers that will appeal to novice beer drinkers as well as ale lovers. These brews prove that fine, handcrafted lagers do exist in the Pacific Northwest.

The tasting room is decorated with photos and memorabilia from turn of the century Roslyn. Look at the pictures of Pennsylvania Avenue and then step outside. Very little has changed over the years – one of the main reasons the town was chosen as the site of "Northern Exposure." After you enjoy the beauty of Roslyn, be sure to visit one of the largest recreation areas in the region, home of the Lemah peaks, located only a few miles away. Lemah, roughly translated, means "the hand" in French, and refers to the five peaks of this mountain – captured in the logo and bottle labels of Roslyn beer.

Ellensburg Brewing Company

505 North Railroad Avenue
Ellensburg WA 98926
509/929-0052

The Ellensburg Brewing Company is located on the outskirts of Ellensburg, a town hidden behind the expansive fields of local farms and ranches. Owner Jerry Thompson operates his brewery in a small brick building.

Ellensburg is home to both Central Washington University and some of the most beautiful stretches of the Yakima River. The history of the town is one of ranching, farming and gold prospecting. And even today, a few people continue to scratch out a living searching for gold. The town's biggest event, the Labor Day Rodeo, is still the time for residents to gather and celebrate the culture of the region.

The brewery captures some of the history and culture in its ales. Swank Creek Gold, a light and pleasing Hefeweizen, shows a prospector panning for gold. Desperado Export Ale, a traditional Strong ale, features two toughs with whiskey bottles and shotguns in hand. The barley wine-style Winter Hawk is graced by a picture of its namesake, a particular species of hawk that winters in the region. All beers are available locally in 12-ounce bottles and on tap at the brewery for tastings. Thompson also brews a root beer, a treat for kids both young and old.

Established: 1994

Hours: Noon-6 pm, Saturday and Sunday

Children: Yes

Food: No

Entertainment: No

Smoking: No

Payment: Checks

Takeout: Yes

Directions: From I-90 heading east, take exit 108 to Ellensburg. After crossing over the freeway, turn right on Dolar Way. Follow the road for about a mile until it curves to the right becoming Railroad Way. Brewery is on the right just before the first main cross street.

Grant's Brewery Pub

32 N. Front Street
Yakima WA 98901
509/575-2922

Grant's Brewery Pub began brewing beer in 1982. For head brewer Bert Grant, whose brewing career began in 1945, the goal has always been to produce high-quality, traditional -styled ales. And, even though the ownership of Grant's has recently changed hands, the Brewery Pub is still Bert's domain, a place to spin out delightfully rich and full-bodied ales.

The pub is located in the north half of the old Yakima train station. The inside of the building has been refinished to create a warm, relaxing pub split into two rooms, separated by a small brewing operation used to produce the cask-conditioned ales served at the pub. The main brewing and bottling is done in a large warehouse on the edge of town. Tours are available by appointment.

The cozy atmosphere of the pub, however, is ideal for sampling Bert Grant's ales. The ales generally are very hoppy, and are served at a temperature that brings out their best characteristics. Grant's Scottish Ale, the flagship product, is a strong, hoppy, traditional ale that tastes even better cask-conditioned. The Perfect Porter and Imperial Stout, the darkest ales, are both thick and rich with varying degrees of chocolate flavor. Grant's India Pale Ale is a light-colored ale with very hoppy bitterness and aroma. While all of Grant's Ales are bottled, the true flavors and delights of the ales really come out when tasted direct from the brewery, in the comfort of the Brewery Pub.

Established: 1982

Hours: 11:30 am-midnight, Monday-Thursday, 11:30 am-1 am, Friday and Saturday, 11:30 am-9 pm Sunday (closed Sundays in winter)

Children: Yes

Food: Standard pub grub

Entertainment: Darts, board games, television, live jazz and blues

Smoking: No

Payment: Checks, Visa/MC

Takeout: Yes

Directions: From I-82, take the First Street exit. Follow all the way into town to Yakima. Turn right on Yakima and then right onto Front Street. Pub is on left in old train depot.

Northern Lights Brewing Company

1701 S. Lawson Road
Airway Heights, WA 99001
509/244-4909

Established: 1993

Hours: 9 am-5 pm
Monday-Saturday

Children: Yes

Food: None

Entertainment: None

Smoking: No

Payment: Checks

Takeout: Yes

Directions: Tours by appointment. Please call for directions.

Northern Lights Brewing Company, located in a big storage building in the Spokane suburb of Airway Heights, makes up in quality ales what it may lack in ambiance. The brewery focuses on draft distribution, and the extent of the entertainment is the music pounding out of brewer Mark Irvin's radio. Look for a new facility in the next year, however, as increased distribution and demand forces Northern Lights to move to more accommodating quarters.

Irvin spent several years working for Hale's, and he has blended the finest of the Hale's traditions with his own to produce six wonderful creations. He lager-conditions all of his ales, letting colder temperatures and time produce smooth, full-bodied ales with deep, complex flavors. The brewery is mostly made up of old dairy equipment which is remarkably well suited for the production of beer.

Lightest of the Northern Lights ales are the Creme Ale and Blueberry Creme Ale. Fermented with huge quantities of Oregon blueberries (instead of extract, an easier and less-flavorful alternative), the Blueberry Creme Ale is an excellent light ale or dessert ale, with the smell and taste of fresh berries. Crystal Bitter, the most popular Northern Lights ale, is a very hoppy Extra Special Bitter-styled ale, dry-hopped for an extra punch of herbal hop aroma and flavor. Chocolate Dunkle, a rich dark ale brewed with plenty of chocolate malt and roasted barley, is simply a wonderful brew. If you visit in winter, look for the Northern Lights Winter Ale, a very hoppy, dark amber brew with a high alcohol content sure to warm you to your toes.

Fort Spokane Brewery
W. 401 Spokane Falls Boulevard
Spokane WA 99201
509/838-3809

The original Fort Spokane Brewery, constructed in 1889, was operated by brothers Bernard and Max Bockemuehl and supplied beer to the U.S. Cavalry troops stationed at the fort. The present-day brewery has revived the traditions of the Bockemuehl brothers and brews a German-style ale known as an Alt. Alt beers ferment at warmer ale temperatures, but then finish in a Lager-like environment. The result is an ale with complex flavors and a clean, smooth finish.

The pub is a marvelous place, located in one of the many turn-of-the-century buildings still standing in downtown Spokane; an original tin-stamped ceiling and an absolutely stunning antique back bar are two of the brewery's charms. The labyrinthine cellars, which house the fermenters, conditioners and kegs, were once the site a Prohibition speakeasy, with tunnels connecting the site to other prominent buildings of the time.

Brewer Brian Johnson produces four standard ales and a series of seasonal products. Flagship ale Border Run, an amber with a smooth, malty flavor, is rivaled in popularity by the seasonal rye, an increasingly fashionable style with a distinctive spicy flavor. Red Alt, a sweet, medium-bodied ale brewed with caramel malts to produce the red color and smooth flavor, is a must try. Bulldog Stout, Godzilla (a "big" India Pale Ale) and an Octoberfest are a few of the other Fort Spokane brews.

The Fort Spokane Brewery, with its distinctive brewing style and beautiful building, is a treat for any fan of microbrewing. The pub is also one of the best places to hear a sampling from Spokane's hot blues scene, offering live music several nights a week.

Established: 1989

Hours: 11 am-midnight Sunday-Thursday, 11 am-2 am Friday and Saturday

Children: Yes

Food: Eclectic lunch and dinner menu

Entertainment:
Television, weekend live blues

Smoking:
Yes

Payment:
Checks,
Visa/MC

Takeout: Yes

Directions: From I-90 in Spokane, take downtown exit and head north to Spokane Falls Blvd. Turn left onto Spokane Falls and go four blocks to Washington. Brewery is on the SW corner of Washington and Spokane Falls.

Birkebeiner Brewing Company

35 W. Main
Spokane WA 99201
509/458-0854

The Birkebeiner Brewery is one of Spokane's newest hotspots. The brewery is located on the right as you walk in. Serving tanks stand above the bar behind glass. The bar offers at least 10 beers at all times. including five lighter ales – a Hefeweizen, Vienna Cream Ale, and Belgian Raspberry. Amusing Alien Amber Ale is a medium-bodied ale with a good balance of malt and hops. For hopheads, the India Pale Ale is the hoppiest of Birkebeiner's offerings. Stout lovers should try the Sasquatch Oatmeal Stout, a thick and creamy brew with light chocolate overtones.

The restaurant is a fresh and somewhat stylish place. Large windows overlooking the street allow passersby a glimpse into the restaurant – marble-topped tables in the bar area, high ceilings, walls decorated with World War I print reproductions and beer advertisements, and comfortable tables and booths.

Birkebeiner Brewing Company

The wonderful food offered in the eclectic restaurant menu makes a perfect complement to Birkebeiner's ales. The menu is a refreshing change from the typical burgers and pizza fare available at many brewpubs and fits well into the style and approach of the Birkebeiner Brewery. Cajun and Mexican influences are evident in many items, including Jambalaya, Seafood Gumbo, Black Bean and Rice Burritos or Chicken Enchiladas with Habenero Bean Sauce.

Established: 1994

Hours: 11:30 am-midnight Monday-Thursday, 11:30 am-2 am Friday and Saturday. Closed Sunday

Children: Yes

Food: Full menu of "international cuisine" foods

Entertainment: Darts, live music

Smoking: No

Payment: Checks, Visa/MC

Takeout: Yes

Directions: From I-90 in Spokane, take the Division Street exit. Head north on Division to Spokane Falls Blvd. Take a left onto Spokane Falls, a left on Brown and a left onto Main.

Hale's Ales (Spokane)

E. 5634 Commerce Street
Spokane, WA 99212
509/534-7553

Hale's Ales, located in a restored three-story, brick schoolhouse, has brewed beer for over a decade, making it an old-timer in the American brewing rebirth. Hale's moved in 1992 from the original brewery in Colville, 70 miles north of Spokane. Movers lifted the brewing equipment through the windows and workers hand-carried grain up to the second floor until the recent addition of a grain silo.

The tasting room is situated halfway between the second and third floors overlooking the brewery. Hale's exclusive use of old, converted dairy tanks and an open fermenting approach allows visitors to watch the beer bubble and grow as it ages. Some ales are available on tap at the tasting room. During the year, the brewery hosts several special events that feature live music and food.

Although Spokane is the original home of Hale's, the city now serves as the company's secondary brewing location, supplying smaller markets like Spokane, Eastern Washington, Idaho and Montana with draft beer. Hale's new Fremont brewery in Seattle (see page 94) produces the majority of the 10,000 barrels brewed annually. The Spokane operation still brews all products; from the Hale's Pale American Ale, the original and still most popular brew, to the Celebration Porter. The brewery also produces a variety of seasonals including an Irish ale, India Pale Ale, Octoberfest ale and the Wee Heavy, a barley wine-style ale.

Established: 1983

Hours: 8am-4 pm Monday-Friday, tours by appointment

Children: Yes

Food: No

Entertainment: Occasional acoustic music

Smoking: No

Payment: Checks

Takeout: Yes

Directions: From I-90 in Spokane, take exit 286 west to Fancher Road. Turn right on Fancher and go about one mile to Commerce. Brewery is on left on the corner.

The Leavenworth Brewery

636 Front Street
Leavenworth, WA 98826
509/548-4545

Established: 1992

Hours: Winter: 11 am-10 pm Sunday-Thursday, 11 am-midnight Friday and Saturday; Summer: 11 am-11 pm Sunday-Thursday, 11 am-midnight Friday and Saturday

Children: Yes, in a special section

Food: Pub fare

Entertainment: Television, darts, live music

Smoking: Yes

Payment: Checks, Visa/MC

Takeout: Yes

Directions: Follow Highway 2 as it passes through the heart of Leavenworth. The brewery is on the south side of the highway, upstairs in a three-story building.

What could be better after enjoying the spectacular outdoors than savoring a brew? Leavenworth Brewing is perfectly located for just that purpose. The pub area is upstairs, and the spiral staircase provides a view of the large copper brew tank as you enter. Seating consists of long common tables situated in the back of the bar area near the entrance. Televisions hang above the bar. The crowd is a nice mix of locals and tourists, and food is primarily burgers and nachos. Entertainment includes live music on weekends and daily brewery tours.

The regular beers on tap include the always popular Whistling Pig Wheat, Escape Altbier, Dirty Face Stout, Friesian Pilsner and Hodgson's India Pale Ale. Past seasonals have included Blind Pig Dunkelweizen, Bull's Tooth Porter, an Oktober Fest and variations on the bock theme.

At the foot of the North Cascades, Leavenworth is a gateway into the mountains from Eastern Washington. In the immediate vicinity are some of the most easily-accessible hiking, mountain-biking, rafting and rock-climbing sites in the state. The area also offers skiing, canoeing and mountaineering of all sorts. The town is built in mock-Bavarian style with a sign "wilkomming" you to an almost theme-land like village. This is tourist heaven and the brewery is a welcome break from the hustle and bustle.

Winthrop Brewing Company

P.O. Box 112
Winthrop, WA 98862
509/996-3183

The Winthrop Brewing Company is set in an old, red schoolhouse, a town that feels like it belongs to the Old West. The funky interior of the brewpub reflects this. It looks like an old saloon with four-inch thick wooden tables and a bar that wouldn't budge if the place were bombed! Note the collections of 600 cigarette lighters and 300 lipstick kisses on the backs of coasters adorning the walls.

Owner Dan Yingling brings a background of brewery apprenticeships and professional training to his craft and has created a line of beers that is wildly popular with the locals. The establishment's standard brews include Outlaw Pale Ale, the local favorite; Hopalong Red Ale; Grampa Clem's Brown Ale and Black Canyon Porter, a full-bodied porter with a smooth, roasty aftertaste. Seasonal brews include Boulder Creek Golden Bock, Grizzly Paw Honey Rye, OktoberWest, Jingle Bell Ale and Uncle Buford's Scottish Ale.

Winthrop is one of those eclectic mountain hideaways that is truly off the beaten path. The North Cascade Highway, a wonderland of hiking, fishing and skiing fun, is closed from the west in the winter, leaving Winthrop somewhat isolated, so the best times to visit are spring or summer.

Established: 1993

Hours: 11 am-midnight Monday-Sunday

Children: Yes

Food: Fish & chips, burgers, pizzas from spent grain

Entertainment: Board games, TV, live music

Smoking: No

Payment: Checks, Visa/MC, Discover

Takeout: Yes

Directions: The brewpub is on Highway 20, on the west side of the road as it passes through town.

Buchanan Brewing Company

821 14th Street
Oroville, WA 98844
509/476-2889

Established: 1996

Hours: 11 am-10 pm
Monday-Sunday

Children: Yes

Food: Pub fare, grilled
chicken dishes, BBQ ribs

Entertainment: Big-
screen TV,
surround-sound stereo

Smoking: Yes

Payment: Visa/MC,
Discover

Takeout: Yes

Directions: From
Highway 97, turn west on
14th. Drive two blocks
and the brewery is on
your right.

This large, new brewery is geared for draft production and distribution. Buchanan Brewing Company is already shipping beer throughout Washington State. Owner/brewer Rick Buchanan and brewer Jerry Oakes are both original Redhook brewers who left during that company's rapid growth period and returned to their roots in Eastern Washington to start their own venture.

The facility features large, twin German copper mash and lauter tuns in the front window. Placing the mash process in the front created elaborate plumbing challenges for Oakes, who had to lay pipes across the long ceiling to move the beer through the large building. The back of the structure features a lagering room for their planned lager beers.

The brewpub occupies the front corner and features a large brick hearth and stove, lending a cozy atmosphere to the small pub space. This is an intimate place for a few friends to enjoy a beer and a plate of orange-garlic glazed chicken or baby-back ribs.

The first beer of the venture is a light Session ale called Triple B or Buchanan's Best Bitter. Future beers will include a Pale Ale and other ales, as well as a line of lagers.

Mac & Jack's, Seattle, WA, 206/868-4778

Mac Renkin and Jack Schrapp, brewing for distribution in the Seattle area since 1994, will soon open a new brewing facility with a tasting room. In addition to African Amber, Jaegerweizen, a Northwest-style Hefeweizen and the Black Jack Porter, all contract-brewed for special accounts, the brewers plan to develop several recipes for the new brewery, starting with an India Pale Ale.

North Sound Brewing, Oak Harbor, WA, 360/679-1960

The North Sound Brewery & Restaurant will be Oak Harbor's second brewpub and the fourth microbrewery on Whidbey Island. It will feature a 10 to 15 barrel brewhouse coupled with a pub and grill-style eatery.

Whidbey Island Brewing, Langley, WA, 360/579-0727

With the opening of their first satellite brewpub in Oak Harbor, Whidbey Island Brewing has begun what promises to be a series of exciting multiple environment brewpubs. Other establishments are planned for the future, with some served by the main brewery in Langley and others brewing on their own. The company models its establishments on the phenomenally successful McMenamins system. Look for the next brewpub soon.

Redmond Brewing Company, Redmond, WA, 206/883-9835

Tom Price, an investor in a Huntington Beach/Laguna Beach chain of brewpubs, plans to launch Redmond's first brewpub in this, his hometown area. This massive operation will be in the heart of downtown Redmond. It will be centered around a brewhouse and clocktower, with various seating areas, a banquet area/concert facility and a bar area decorated with etched glass, bricks and hardwood floors. Initial offerings will be an American Pale Ale and an Amber Lager. Plans include authentic German ales served in tulip glasses with flavored syrups on the side and cask-conditioned beers. The menu will include gourmet wood-fired pizzas, salads, sandwiches and pastas.

Elysian Brewing Company & Public House,
1221 Pike Street, Seattle, WA, 206/860-1920

The Elysian Brewing Company, a blend of brewpub and distribution-focused microbrewery, plans to offer an Extra Special Bitter, a Maibock and a stout, followed by a pilsner or a Dortmunder. Dick

Cantwell, head brewer/partner will brew a line of 15 to 20 beers. The brewpub will be in a large nouveau-industrial building on Capitol Hill, offering a medium-priced menu of items ranging from potpies to sausages to Thai noodle salad. An outdoor deck will feature an urban view of the Seattle skyline.

North Fork Brewpub

The highway from Bellingham to Mount Baker will soon have a brewpub – the perfect place for a stop on a skiing or hiking trip. To be located between the towns of Deming and Kendall, this tavern-like establishment will serve New York-style pizzas. Owner/brewer Sandy Savage took brewing classes at both UC Davis and Seibel, and brewed for years at Triple Rock Brewery in Northern California. He'll be brewing on a 3½-barrel system, with old grundies and dairy tanks.

North Cascades Brewing Company, 1410 Poke Road, Bellingham, WA, 360/384-0268

Bellingham will soon have a new draft microbrewery. Loretta and Bryan Sheldon are manufacturing and salvaging all the equipment themselves for this 25-barrel brewery near the airport. They'll brew unfiltered, top-fermented ales, called Lowefield Ales, and will start with a true-to-style Extra Special Bitter. Future brews will include a porter, a stout, a Wee Heavy and a bitter.

Snipes Mountain Brewing, P.O. Box 274, Sunnyside, WA 98944, 509/837-2739

Sunnyside, Washington, will soon have its own brewery. Snipes Mountain Brewing, Inc., will be located on Highway 12 (the Yakima Valley Highway) in Sunnyside, at its intersection with 9th Street. Owner Marianne Bliesner says brewmaster Keith Parker, a self-trained home brewer, will start the establishment off with four or five ales. The company will operate a microbrewery shipping beers out to both the draft and bottled markets and will also have a brewpub with a full menu of pub fare.

Virtual Tours

Growing nearly as fast as the microbrewing industry itself is the wealth of information about beers and brewing on the Internet and specifically, the World Wide Web. The Web, a collection of useful information on every topic imaginable, has quickly become the place to learn about the ever-expanding home-brewing and microbrewing renaissance.

The microbrewers of the Pacific Northwest have embraced the World Wide Web as a means to publicize their beers and their brewing techniques. Regional craft beer enthusiasts use the Web to share a variety of reviews and guides to Pacific Northwest brews. Beer and brewing magazines publish articles about Northwest brewing trends, openings, trade gossip and other tidbits of Northwest brewing culture. This is where homebrewers publish and exchange recipes, brewpubs announce brews on tap and breweries sell hats, shirts and tell the history of their companies. If you want to know about beer, look no further than your computer screen.

An excellent jumping off point for a virtual tour of Pacific Northwest brewing is the World Wide Web Virtual Library's Beer and Brewing Index located at:

http://www.mindspring.com/~jlock/wwwbeer.html

The Beer and Brewing Index offers dozens of virtual beer guides, including several of the Pacific Northwest. You move from Web site to Web site (referred to as "pages") by simply pointing your cursor on the information you want to get and clicking with your mouse.

The Beer and Brewing Index offers links to the Northwest Brew Page, maintained by Donald Scheidt at:

http://www.teleport.com/~dgs1300/index.shtml

The Northwest Brew Page has extensive listings and reviews of Washington and Oregon breweries, brewpubs, and taverns.

The Oregon Brew Page, is located at:

http://www.teleport.com/~edl/orbeer.html

It is beer enthusiast Ed Lingel's contribution to virtual touring of Pacific Northwest breweries. Lingel provides additional links to brewpub and brewery Web pages, as well as the Web site for the Oregon Brewers Guild, a membership organization for the craft brewers of Oregon, at:

http://www.teleport.com/~beer

The Oregon Brewers Guild page includes the complete Microbreweries of Oregon Guide published by the Guild in 1995. The guide offers maps to the breweries as well as concise information from the breweries themselves.

The ultimate goal of the virtual tour of Pacific Northwest microbreweries is to visit the individual brewery sites. The Oregon Brew Page, Northwest Brew Page, Beer and Brewing Index and other Web resources provide direct links to brewery Web pages.

Three Pacific Northwest brewing operations stand out as representative of what is best about brewery Web sites. The Okanagan Spring Brewery of British Columbia (see page 160) shares detailed information about their beers at:

http://www.okspring.com.

The Oregon Fields Brewing Company (see page 28) Web page:

http://surf.rio.com/~fields/fields.html

It offers one of the best virtual tours brewing operations to be found. Brewer David Sohigian takes you through each step of the brewing process with photographs and links to additional information about how to make beer. Pyramid Breweries, Inc. (see page 95), makers of Pyramid Ales and Thomas Kemper Lagers, has developed a visually stunning and very humorous Web page at:

http://www.hartbrew.com

Visitors can play darts, write on the bathroom walls, read what other visitors have said about strange food habits or learn about the proper care and serving of Pyramid Breweries, Inc. brews.

Going on a virtual tour of the breweries is obviously not as much fun as actually being there; after all, you can't download the beer! But to learn more about your favorite pub, uncover information about new places or to learn about happenings in the microbrew industry, the World Wide Web is an excellent and constantly expanding resource.

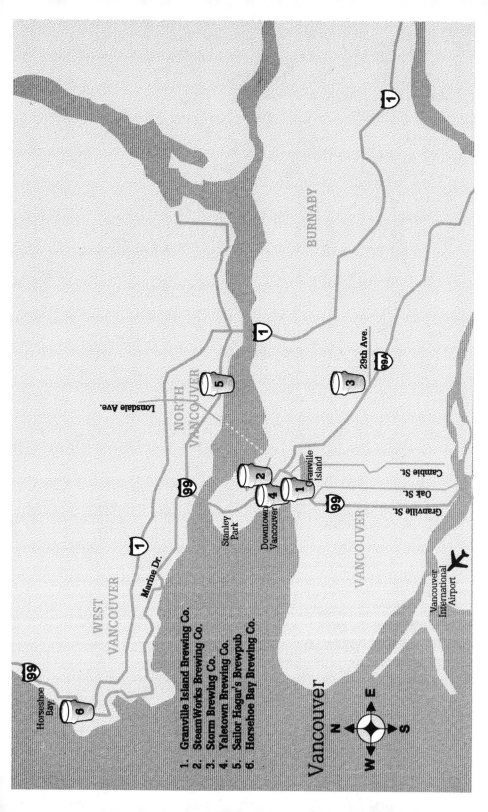

Vancouver

1. Granville Island Brewing Co.
2. SteamWorks Brewing Co.
3. Storm Brewing Co.
4. Yaletown Brewing Co.
5. Sailor Hagar's Brewpub
6. Horseshoe Bay Brewing Co.

BRITISH COLUMBIA

B ritish Columbia's microbrewing revolution is dominated by the smooth, enjoyable flavors of lagers. Rare in
Oregon or Washington, lagers are brewed slowly in
much colder temperatures than ales and are the staple among
BC's brew enthusiasts. While ales are produced by a handful
of brewers around the province, traditionally styled lagers,
many based on recipes from the turn of the century, still hold
sway with drinkers and brewers alike.

Brewing regulations may be part of the reason for the abundance of lagers. By law, microbreweries in BC may sell on
draft or in bottles, but not through a brewpub. In order to be
competitive in this situation, brewers try to reach as large a
market as possible. Brewpubs, however, can only sell in-
house and tend to favor the "bigger" tastes of ales. The
gradual growth of brewpubs and the enormous popularity of
homebrewing guarantee that interest in ales will continue to
grow.

While the city of Vancouver has the highest concentration of
breweries and brewpubs, brewing establishments dot the BC
landscape. The diverse beauty and outdoor adventures available throughout the province are the perfect complement to
a sampling adventure in BC's growing microbrewing culture.

Shaftebury Brewing
7989 82nd Street
Delta, BC V4G 1L7
604/940-2887

Shaftebury was founded in East Vancouver in 1987 by Tim Wittig and Paul Beaton, two college students waiting tables and wondering what to do next. They are still the sole owners of this microbrewery, which has grown to become BC's third largest. Neither had a brewing background, but they were impressed with the concept of a small-sized brewing venture. So they hired Spinnakers' original brewer to teach them how to brew and never looked back.

The company's success is evident in the brand new plant in Delta, where it mashes 105 hecto-liter batches (approximately 90 barrels) in handsome new mash and lauter tuns. The beer is fermented in seven towering unitanks and several smaller ones. The brewery still uses salvaged bottling and kegging equipment, though, lending the massive operation a touch of charm. The retail store offers a wide array of beer paraphernalia, as well as the full line of beers to go. Brewery tours are offered regularly.

Shaftebury beers are all mild and malty and include a slightly sweet and light-bodied Honey Pale Ale, a lightly-hopped Rainforest Amber Ale and the enigmatic dark Cream Ale, with a nutty flavor from the roasted malt. A Christmas Ale is the winter season brew. Their beers, bearing splashy labels proclaiming "Think Globally, Drink Locally," are distributed in kegs and bottles throughout the lower mainland and Whistler areas, as well as on Vancouver Island and will also appear in Northwest Washington before too long.

Established: 1995

Hours: 10 am-6 pm
Monday-Sunday

Children: Yes

Food: No

Entertainment: No

Smoking: No

Payment: Visa/MC, Interac

Takeout: Yes

Directions: From 99, take the Tsawassen River Road exit and head east on River Road. Drive approximately three miles to 82nd Street. The brewery is on your right.

Russell Brewing
Unit 202, 13018 80th Avenue
Surrey, BC V3W 3A8
604/599-1190

Russell Brewing is one of Canada's only family-owned cottage breweries and was launched by the Russell brothers with a little help from their relatives. The company is quite successful, producing about 300 kegs per month, for distribution all over lower mainland BC. Currently there is no retail store and no regular brewery tours, but you can arrange for one by calling ahead.

The brewery equipment is brand new and shiny, including a 20-hectoliter (17-barrel) open-fermentation system and four conditioning tanks in a cooler for lagering ales. This allows the brewers to achieve that unparalleled level of smoothness associated with cold-conditioning.

Before he and his brother opened their brewery, Mark Russell was a long-time brewer at Granville Island Brewing (see page 142). At Russell Brewing he brews traditional British- style ales, with British yeast and imported British malts. To suit the Canadian palate, the beers are filtered for clarity and aged for fairly long periods of time – often a month in the cold room.

Two standard offerings are a medium-hopped Amber ale that is light in color, but not in body or flavor, and a Cream ale that you've got to taste to believe. This dark cream ale is an excellent beer in terms of complex malt flavors, smoothness and drinkability. Future brews will include a Christmas ale and a Lemon ale.

Established: 1995

Hours: Call to arrange a tour

Children: Yes

Food: No

Entertainment: No

Smoking: No

Payment: Cash only

Takeout: No

Directions: From 91 (Annacis Highway), take the 72nd Street exit and follow 72nd east to 99A (King George Highway). From 99, turn north on 99A (King George Highway). From 99A,e turn west on 80th Street. Follow 80th to the intersection with 132nd. Cross 132nd and take the next left. The brewery is in the second white building on the left.

Pure and Natural Cottage Ales · RUSSELL BREWING COMPANY · Family Brewed in British Columbia

VANCOUVER
BRITISH
COLUMBIA

The city of Vancouver is the focus of a sprawling region known as the Lower Mainland. The majestic drive up Highway 99 to Whistler delineates the area's northeast boundary, and the great Fraser Valley draws the southern border. Vancouver is nestled between the Strait of Georgia, busy with ocean-bound freighters, and the Lillooet Range, the continuation of Oregon and Washington's Cascade Mountains. This expansive metro area serves as a nexus for international trade and is home to an equally metropolitan population of beer drinkers.

The Vancouver region is the birth place of British Columbia's current microbrewing renaissance. Horseshoe Bay Brewing opened in 1982 in West Vancouver, followed by Spinnakers Brewpub in 1983 and Granville Island Brewing Company in 1984. The local drinkers here were slower to catch on to microbrewed beers than in Seattle and Portland, however, and many of the early breweries and pubs failed. The result of these closures is the slower and more cautious growth of the BC brewing industry.

The metro area's brewing scene resembles Seattle in the early 1990s – only a handful of brewpubs, but a number of draft breweries. Recent years have seen many new operations open in the area, including several new brewpubs. Yaletown Brewing Company and Sailor Hagar's Brewpub both opened in 1994, followed by

SteamWorks Brewing Company in 1995. These establishments have proven wildly popular, and indicate a growing enthusiasm for brewpub in general and also for the hearty flavors of ales. This is a shift from the deeply rooted tradition of lagering in Vancouver.

The proper brew tour of Vancouver has three parts. First, spend your evenings relaxing in the region's brewpubs. Second, take advantage of the informative tours conducted by the city's microbreweries. Many of the larger operations, such as Shaftebury Brewing or Vancouver Island Brewing, offer regular brewery tours which usually include a tasting. Finally, visit the local taverns. Due to the predominance of breweries in Vancouver and regulations enforcing a strict division between brewpubs and breweries (see British Columbia, page 135), the "alehouse," much like in Seattle, is quickly becoming the best place to sample the diverse, hand-crafted brews produced around the city.

British
Columbia

N
W E
S

100 Miles

Bowen Island
   Bowen Island Brewing Co. Ltd.
Delta
   Shaftsbury Brewing
Kamloops
   Bear Brewing Co.
Kelowna
   Tree Brewing Company
   Black Mountain Brewpub/
   Schoolhouse Cafe
Nanaimo
   Bastion Brewing
Nelson
   Nelson Brewing Co.
North Vancouver
   Sailor Hagar's Brewpub
Penticton
   Tin Whistle Brewing Company
Squamish
   Tall Ship Ale Brewing Co.
Surrey
   Russell Brewing
Vancouver
   (See map, page 141)
Vernon
   Okanagon Spring Brewery
Victoria
   Spinnakers Brewpub
   Swans Hotel/Buckerfield's Brewery
   Vancouver Island Brewing Co.
Whistler
   Whistler Brewing Co.

16

Prince George

97

16

VANCOUVER ISLAND

99 Whistler

Squamish

Kamloops

Vernon

Kelowna

1

1

1

5

Nelson

Penticton

3

Bowen
Island
Nanaimo

Vancouver
Surrey
Delta

Victoria
Anacortes

5

WASHINGTON

Granville Island Brewing Company

1441 Cartwright Street, Granville Island, Vancouver, BC V6H 3R7
604/687-2739

Granville Island Brewing Company occupies most of a large building. The front corner is a retail store, well-stocked with all types of beer paraphernalia. An impressive, two-story brewing system towers in the main area. The brewery, conceived by Vancouver businessman Mitch Taylor, was opened more than a decade ago. The company's first beer, Island Lager, a Bavarian-style pilsner, was the result of his desire to locally brew German pilsners.

The next offering was Lord Granville Pale Ale, followed in turn by Island Bock and Island Light. Next came Canada's first micro in a can, cold-filtered Natural Draft. The brewery marked its first decade with a 10th Anniversary Ale. Granville Island Brewing is now one of BC's largest regional breweries, with a major brewing facility in Kelowna and distribution throughout the province.

Granville Island is a must-see part of Vancouver. Tucked away below the bridge over the bay, the island bustles with a Euro-style open-air market by day and restaurants and an island theater company by night. The island is quite small and an interesting mix of industrial, craft and retail businesses strung along the waterfront. For a perfect outing, visit the brewery, then stroll through the market, grab a bite to eat, and finish the night off with a show at the theater.

Established: 1984

Hours: Retail store: 9 am-7 pm Monday-Sunday

Children: Yes

Food: No

Entertainment: No

Smoking: No

Payment: Visa/MC, Am Ex

Takeout: Yes

Directions: Follow Highway 99 as it heads north to downtown Vancouver. Follow the turn-off sign to Granville Island just before the bridge to downtown. From Highway 1, take the Grandview Highway exit. Follow 12th Avenue to Hemlock. Turn right on Hemlock and follow signs to Granville Island. When you pull onto the island, go right and the brewery is on your left.

SteamWorks Brewing Company
375 Water Street
Vancouver, BC V6B 5C6
604/689-2739

SteamWorks is an outstanding downtown Vancouver destination, featuring different settings in the ground floor and basement of The Landing on Vancouver's waterfront. Its downtown location and access to city transportation makes this a perfect stopping point on any tour of the city.

The Landing is the largest heavy timber-constructed building in Western Canada. The original massive wooden beams are still visible inside, and the walls feature beautiful new wainscoting. A trip down the central spiral staircase leads to the pub, which has a fireplace, pool tables and a dimly lit restaurant. The fermenters are separated from the dining area by a wrought-iron fence, and the 10-barrel brewhouse is set behind glass at the restaurant's rear. The brewery is called SteamWorks because the heat for the brewing kettle comes from a tap into the city's steam lines.

The savory menu, described by manager Thain Campbell as "Pacific Northwest comfort food," offers wood-fired pizzas, black bean cakes, onion tarts and jambalaya. The daily specials are outstanding.

Brewer Shirley Warne comes to SteamWorks from the large brewpubs of Eastern Canada. Her English-style standards are Harvest Amber Ale, a Nutbrown ale and the Not-So-Pale Ale. An eclectic array of seasonals includes Earthquake Dopplebock, an India Pale Ale, a Scotch, a wheat, an Octoberfest, a stout, a Sour Cherry Ale and a Four Berry Ale.

Established: 1995

Hours: 11:30 am-1 am Monday-Saturday, 11:30 am-midnight Sunday

Children: Yes, in the restaurant

Food: Casual and fine dining

Entertainment: Pool, library, televisions, live jazz 2 pm-5 pm, Saturday and Sunday

Smoking: Yes, in the pub. No, in the restaurant

Payment: Visa/MC, Am Ex

Takeout: No

Directions: Follow 99 across Granville Island into the heart of downtown Vancouver, where it becomes Seymour Street. Follow Seymour until it ends at Hastings. Go right one block, then left to the beginning of Water Street. The brewpub is on your left.

Storm Brewing Company

310 Commercial Drive
Vancouver, BC V5L 3V6
604/255-9119

Established: 1995

Hours: Tours by appointment

Children: No

Food: No

Entertainment: No

Smoking: No

Payment: N/A

Takeout: No

Directions: Call for directions.

Storm Brewing, Vancouver's youngest and smallest microbrewery, is one of the city's best-kept secrets and is an example of minimalist quality brewing at its finest. Brewer James Walton, with a personal background in homebrewing and welding, is a natural commercial brewer – though certainly not a typical one. The brewery consists of a combination old pharmaceutical, dairy and pulp mill equipment that is not much to look at, but it works magic under Walton's careful crafting.

Beers are available on tap throughout Vancouver proper, but strictly within the city limits. They are well worth seeking out – look for the distinctive metal tap handles that are vaguely reminiscent of electrical coils.

It's a rare treat to find a brewery attempting a true Alt style, and the Red Sky Altbier fits the bill. The complexities derived by the use of the seven malts yield sublime subtleties, and the full hop aroma with its floral highlights hovers in the nose.
Walton also brews a medium-bodied Midnight Porter, aptly named for its color. His richest beer, however, is Espressale, a brown ale with a large amount of espresso added after the wort has fermented. Seasonals have included an India Pale Ale and an Orange Lambic, which is an outrageous twist on Lambic traditions and also outrageously good.

Yaletown Brewing Company

1111 Mainland Street
Vancouver, BC V6B 2T9
604/681-2739

Established: 1994

Hours: 11:30 am-midnight Sunday-Wednesday, 11:30 am-1 am Thursday-Saturday

Children: Yes, in the restaurant

Food: Full menu of nouveau pub fare

This is Vancouver's premier brewpub and serves as the anchor establishment for the trendy Yaletown district. Yaletown Brewing Company's brewpub is located in one of the neighborhood's converted warehouses and is divided into a pub on the left and a restaurant on the right. The pub has a long, handsome bar, pool tables and dart lanes and a large Mexican sandstone fireplace and hearth. The brewhouse is visible through the rear glass wall.

The restaurant is adorned with handsome paintings done by a local artist who once lived in the old warehouse. By day the place is bright and cheery, and by night, it's bustling. In nice weather, there is extensive outdoor seating. Menu offerings include wood-fired pizzas, tempting pastas, pound-sized T-bone steaks, seafood and pub fare, such as fried green tomatoes, beer-battered artichoke hearts and blackened chicken burgers.

The brewhouse features a 10-hectoliter system (approximately eight barrels), with three closed fermenters and 18 conditioning tanks. Brewmaster Ian Hill, formerly of Shaftebury (see page 137), is an experimental brewer whose recipes change according to customer feedback. Standards include the Munich-style Mainland Lager, bitter with a hint of peat; Indian Arm Pale Ale, named for Indian Arm Bay; a pilsner-style Harbour Light Lager; and a rich, charcoaly stout. Seasonals include an India Pale Ale, a Dunkel, a Smoked Lager, and Old Hooligan's Christmas Ale – tart, fruity and brewed with juniper berries. The bar pours the brews from beer engines for Continental-style sipping pleasure.

Entertainment: Televisions, pool, darts, club dancing Thursday-Saturday

Smoking: Yes, in the pub. No, in the restaurant

Payment: Visa/MC, Am Ex

Takeout: No

Directions: From Highway 99, cross Oak Street Bridge, take first right down to Cambie. Turn left on Cambie and follow it across the Cambie Street Bridge. Turn left on Mainland. Drive two blocks and the brewpub is on the right, on the corner of Mainland and Helmcken.

British Columbia 145

Sailor Hagar's Brewpub
Semisch and First

North Vancouver, BC V7M 3H8
604/984-3087

Sailor Hagar's is North Vancouver's only brewpub and is an excellent destination for the brew tourist. A SeaBus ride over to North Van is worth the trip for this fine establishment alone. The pub sits atop a hill overlooking the water between North Vancouver and down-town, with a panoramic view of the city from inside the pub or out on the spacious wrap-around deck. The interior is decorated lavishly with sail-ing accouterments and oak and brass fixtures. Be sure to note the bas-relief carved dolphins over the fireplace.

The menu offers the usual burgers and fish and chips, but also features some un-usual options, like the peanut satay chicken pizza, chicken strips coated in the brewery's grist and the Scandinavian Platter.

Brewer Gary Lohin is a self-trained home-brewer who convinced owner Al Riedlinger to install the brewhouse next door to his existing neighborhood pub. Since the four fermenters and assorted ale and lager conditioning tanks were installed, Lohin has been brewing a wide variety of unfiltered beers. Regulars include Hägar's Honey Pilsner, Scandinavian Amber Lager, Narwhal Pale Ale, John's Extra Special Bitter, a Belgian Wit brewed with coriander and orange peel and the outstanding Grizzly Nutbrown. Past seasonals include the IRA (India Red Ale), a Maple Oatmeal stout, a Maibock, a Wee Heavy with distinct peat flavor and a Spiced Blueberry wheat. Beers are served both on tap and from a beer engine. The brewhouse is in a separate building from the pub and tours are conducted on request.

Established: 1994

Hours: 11 am-midnight daily

Children: No

Food: Extensive pub fare with a Norwegian flare

Entertainment: Darts, television

Smoking: Yes

Payment: Visa/MC, Am Ex, Interac

Takeout: Yes

Directions: From the SeaBus, walk straight off the dock up the hill three blocks. From 99 take the first exit on the north side of the Lion's Gate Bridge. Stay in the right lane as it loops under the highway. As you head into North Vancouver, take Low Level Road, and take the left fork, Marine Drive, around the hill by the railroad tracks. Now you're on Esplanade. Follow Esplanade across Lonsdale and turn right on Semische. Drive two blocks and the brewpub is on your right.

Horseshoe Bay Brewing Company

6695 Nelson Avenue
West Vancouver, BC V7W 2B2
604/921-8112

Established: 1982

Hours: 10 am-6 pm
Monday-Saturday. Tours
on request

Children: Yes

Food: No

Entertainment: No

Smoking: No

Payment: Checks

Takeout: Kegs only

Directions: From
Highway 99, take the
Horseshoe Bay exit. The
road heads west, then
bears right down a hill,
then jogs right and then
left again downhill
toward the water.
(Ignore the sign
for the ferries
half-way down.)
When you reach
the water, turn
left and go to
the Boathouse
restaurant. The
brewery is behind the
restaurant in the building
on the pier.

Horseshoe Bay is Canada's oldest micro-brewery. Since 1982 it has been a brewpub, a bottling operation and is now strictly producing beers on draft for regional taverns.

This is one of BC's only unfiltered ale breweries and produces four standard brews. Marathon Pale Ale, a Canadian-style, very pale, lightly hopped ale; a Nutbrown ale with more of a smoky flavor than a nutty one, owing to the practice of searing the mash on the bottom of the kettle; Horseshoe Bay Ale, an amber; and a Triple Frambozen, brewed to 7% alcohol. Past seasonals have included a dark brown Christmas Ale, a Cream ale and a pilsner.

The brewery also supplies two local restaurants with whole tanks of beer. At the Raven Pub in Deep Cove, look for the Quarry Rock Pale Ale, and at Ya-Ya's in Horseshoe Bay, the Nutbrown Oyster Ale.

The brewery's setting is lovely – right on the water in the cozy village of Horseshoe Bay, the starting point for ferry rides to Bowen Island, Nanaimo and the northern BC Coast. The hills rise majestically straight out of the water here at the beginning of the stretch of Highway 99 known as the "Sea to Sky Highway."

Bowen Island Brewing Company Ltd.
Artisan Lane
Bowen Island, BC V0N 1G0
604/947-0822

Established: 1994

Hours: Noon-6 pm daily, or call to arrange a tour

Children: Yes

Food: No

Entertainment: No

Smoking: No

Payment: Visa/MC, Interac

Takeout: Yes

Directions: From the ferry dock, drive through the village and up the hill beyond. Just before the crest of the hill, there is a school, then a turn-off to the left with a sign for the brewery. Turn left and drive up the hill. The brewery is on the right.

Bowen Island is the secluded home of one of BC's few English-style breweries. Though the beers are filtered for the finicky Canadian market, they are brewed in open fermentation tanks with traditional top-fermenting yeast. And what a setting! The ferry ride over is just long enough to get a view of the inlet reaching North toward Squamish and the islands scattered around the Sound.

The brewery is comprised of two areas. The retail shop is lined with shelves full of beer paraphernalia and products containing beer. The tidy brewing area is complete with six fermenters and a 27-hectoliter (approximately 23-barrels) brewing system.

The ales brewed here bear some resemblance to their British forebearers, despite the reduction in complexity caused by filtering them. Beers are available in bottles and kegs throughout BC. Look for Bowen Ale, a medium-range simple ale that is light on both the hops and the malt flavors; Blonde Ale, suitable for a hot summer day; Special Bitter, with nice frontal hop aroma and flavorful malts and fruit esters; and Winter Ale, brewed with Oregon bing cherries and a hint of chocolate malts.

Bowen Island also brews for an upscale BC restaurant chain known as Earl's. The standard brew here is Albino Rhino, a simple pale ale. The four seasonal brews are also available.

Tall Ship Ale Company Limited
39002-E Discovery Way
Squamish, BC V0N 3G0
604/892-5696

Established: 1994

Hours: Noon-6 pm Tuesday-Sunday. Regular tours on the weekends

Children: Yes

Food: No

Entertainment: No

Smoking: No

Payment: Visa/MC, Interac

Takeout: Yes

With the recent addition of its retail store and tasting room, Tall Ship Ales is an excellent stopping point between Vancouver and Whistler. Dave Philip and Bill Herman, avid homebrewers with plenty of drive and some professional training from the Seibel Institute, brew top-fermented ales, lagering them at cold temperatures to produce a distinct smoothness.

The micro-filtered beers come in 16-ounce bottles, a traditional U.S. pint, but an untraditional bottle size. They are also coming out with a barley wine, called Three Sheats to the Wind, and a Black Raspberry Porter in 7-ounce bottles. The bottled beers are available throughout BC and are also shipped to Japan. The flagship brew, Tall Ship Ale, is also available in kegs. Tall Ship Ale is smooth with a full hops aroma and flavor stemming from the dry-hopping process. Other brews include the Tall Ship Raspberry Ale, an excellent example of a traditional berry ale; Black Ship Ale, a rich, chocolatey brew with complex malts and a smooth finish; and a Smoked porter, a Rauchbier-styled ale brewed with beechwood-smoked malts that give this malty, robust brew a delightful finish.

Directions: From Highway 99, turn west into the Squamish Industrial Park one kilometer north of the town of Squamish. After you enter the complex, take the first right onto Discovery Way. The brewery is on your right.

The town of Squamish, Tall Ship's home, is half-way up the majestic "Sea to Sky" portion of Highway 99, at the mouth of the long inlet that reaches north from the Sound and beneath the Diamond Head mountains.

Whistler Brewing Company

1209 Alpha Lake Road
Whistler, BC V0N 1B1
604/932-6185

Established: 1989

Hours: Noon-6 pm Tuesday-Friday, 10 am-5 pm Saturday. Tours at 2 pm and 4 pm

Children: Yes

Food: No

Entertainment: No

Smoking: No

Payment: Visa/MC, Interac

Takeout: Yes

Directions: From Highway 99, turn west at Function Junction onto Alpha Lake Road two kilometers south of the town of Whistler. Cross the railroad tracks and the brewery is the second building on the right. (Note: There is also a road called Alta Lake Road heading west from 99 at the south end of town. These roads are not the same.)

Whistler Brewing Company is one of BC's largest microbreweries, located in the tourist heaven of the peak of the "Sea to Sky" stretch of Highway 99. The mountains are breathtaking here, with Whistler Mountain looming over the entire area, and such smaller, though equally impressive mountains as Black Tusk completing the high alpine feel of the area.

The brewery includes a handsome new retail store and tasting room with all the Whistler beers on tap. This is an excellent stop for skiers or mountaineers looking for a refreshing lager. A tour of the place is a mind-boggling hodge-podge of old and new, from Europe and North America and includes a handsome pair of copper mash and lauter tuns built in 1954 and acquired from the Mössingen Brewery in Germany.

True to Canadian tradition, Whistler brews strictly bottom-fermenting lagers, though their labels have included the word "ale" in the past. The brewery is now in the process of changing the names back. Whistler's Dunkel lager, originally known as Black Tusk Ale, will soon be labeled simply, Black Tusk. This beer, first released in 1990, achieved its current porter-like flavor in 1993, when the recipe was changed to endow it with a malty character ending in a full hops celebration. The brewery's first beer, Whistler Premium Lager, is a golden German lager. Whistler's Mother "Pale Ale" is a lager that is truly similar to an American Pale Ale, with a floral aroma and a touch of caramel.

Buckerfield's Brewery/Swan Hotel

506 Pandora Avenue
Victoria, BC V8W 1N6
604/361-3310 or 800/668-7926

Established: 1989

Hours: 7 am-11 am daily, 11:30 am-2 am Monday-Saturday, 11:30 am-midnight Sunday

Children: Yes

Food: Full menu breakfast, lunch and dinner

This charming building, situated on the water near downtown amid shops, businesses and some industrial buildings, was once a granary. The elegant brewpub occupies the front section of the bottom floor; the brewery itself is in the back section.

Buckerfield's uses only imported British malts, and brews an impressive line of non-filtered beers. The standard choices are Arctic Ale, Buckerfield's Bitter, Pandora Pale Ale, Swan's Oatmeal Stout, Appleton Brown Ale, Old Towne Bavarian Lager and Riley's Scotch Ale. The Oatmeal stout is particularly good, with rounded roasted flavors, and Buckerfield's Bitter is a wonderfully hoppy brew without that astringent bite.

The Swan's Pub, with its woodwork and wainscoting, is an excellent example of old-world British ambiance. This "feel" is often captured in BC's brewpubs. But the artwork displayed throughout the pub, produced by local, contemporary artists, imbues the establishment with a distinctly modern quality. In keeping with other BC brewpubs, the beer is served both on cold taps and beer engines. Sipping a barely-carbonated, cellar-temperature Appleton Brown Ale is about as European as it gets in North America.

The restaurant is a fine dining establishment, offering an extensive selection of seafood, from trout to oysters, a similarly varied list of pastas, and a collection of medium-priced, finely-prepared entrees. The Swan Hotel offers travelers deluxe, executive suite-style accommodations in close proximity to the heart of the city. Most of the 29 suites are suitable for six people and include dining areas, private patios, terraces and skylights.

Entertainment: Live blues and jazz Thursday through Sunday

Smoking: Yes, in separate rooms

Payment: Visa/MC, Am Ex, Diners Club, Interac

Takeout: Yes

Directions: From the ferries, take highway 17 into Vancouver, where it becomes Blanshard. Turn right on Pandora Avenue. Go five blocks to store. The hotel and brewery are on the corner.

Spinnakers Brewpub

308 Catherine Street
Victoria, BC V8W 2S9
604/386-2739

Spinnakers, Canada's oldest brewpub of the current microbrewery renaissance, sits on the water at the edge of Victoria. The building is aristocratic and features classic Victorian architecture and traditional British pub woodwork. Upstairs is a traditional taproom, with a large common area and a smaller room overlooking the water. The taproom is self-service: Serve yourself a beverage, tell the cook what you want to eat and play the piano if you like. Downstairs is a large, split-level restaurant with a fireplace in the center.

The taproom food is traditional coastal pub fare and includes sandwiches, brewery bread, oysters and calamari. The restaurant's menu is more sophisticated, though still homey, with French toast and fish cakes for breakfast, and such dinner specialties as Cajun Halibut, Highland Beef and a curry of the day.

As with most brewpubs in BC, beers are served both on cold taps and on cellar-temperature beer engines. Some of the most memorable ales are Spinnaker Ale, a malty light ale with delightful fruit esters; a lovely Mild Brown with a soft texture and subtle chocolate malts; a nicely-balanced Oatmeal stout with a sweet finish; and a riotously good barley wine. When fresh, local, organically grown berries are in season, look for such delights as Cranberry Hefeweizen and Blueberry Weizen.

A gentle lawn leads from Spinnakers, down to the harbor-front path. For an enjoyable stroll, follow this winding trail into downtown, just a 10-minute walk away.

Established: 1984

Hours: 7 am-11 pm
Sunday-Saturday

Children: Yes, upstairs in the taproom

Food: Downstairs-casual fine dining; upstairs-a wide range of pub fare

Entertainment: Live acoustic music, especially jazz

Smoking: Yes, in separate rooms

Payment: Visa/MC, Am Ex, Bank Interac

Takeout: Yes

Directions:
From either ferry dock, take Highway 17 into Victoria. After you pass two shopping centers on the right, 17 becomes Blanshard Avenue. Follow Blanshard to Bay Street. Turn right on Bay Street and go over the bridge. Bay ends at a diagonal intersection with Catherine. Turn left on Catherine, cross over Esquimault Street and brewpub is on the right at the end of the street.

Vancouver Island Brewing Company
2330 Government Street
Victoria, BC V8T 5G5
604/361-0007

Vancouver Island is Victoria's only microbrewery. Located in a new, modern facility at the edge of downtown, this brewery produces a sizable output of beer for the local and regional marketplace. With distribution now reaching the lower BC mainland, and soon spreading down to Washington and California, the brewery is poised to become one of BC's foremost regional breweries.

Tours are offered regularly, but call ahead for a reservation and time. The spacious interior houses a two-story system, a sizable bottling area, and a classy tasting room (offering the brewery's wares on draft) overlooking the retail store. The enormous mash tun and kettle are very handsome and are fully computerized.

The beer line consists of Victoria Lager, Hermann's Bavarian Dark Lager, Piper's Pale Ale, a hoppy, zesty medium-bodied ale, and Victoria Weizen, which has a true weiss flavor resulting from authentic German yeast. The winter holiday brew is a triple bock called Hermanator. Vancouver Island is one of the few full-scale, single-location microbreweries offering both ales and lagers. The beers tend to be big and malty, earning head brewer Don Harmes the nickname, "Dr. Malt."

The brewery's location makes it an ideal stop between the two brewpubs in Victoria, Buckerfield's Brewery (see page 151), located on the waterfront a few blocks from Vancouver Island Brewing, and Spinnakers (see page 152), on the road into town from the ferry landing.

Established: 1984

Hours: Tours: 1 pm and 3 pm Wednesday-Saturday; Retail Store: 11 am-6 pm Monday-Thursday, 11 am-7 pm Friday and Saturday

Children: Yes

Food: No

Entertainment: No

Smoking: No

Payment: Visa/MC, Am Ex, Interac

Takeout: Yes

Directions: From the ferries, take Highway 17 into Victoria, where it becomes Blanshard. Pass two shopping centers and turn right on Bay Street. Turn left on Government and the brewery is on your right, half a block down.

Bastion Brewing Company

50 Commercial Street
Nanaimo, BC V9R 5G4
604/754-2448

Bastion Brewing is the domain of owner/brewer Bill Eaton, a refugee from California. A homebrewer and winemaker for years, Eaton and his partner Bruce Samson currently distribute draft beers in the central Vancouver Island area. They hope to expand operations soon to include bottling.

Bastion is the first brewery in the blue collar town of Nanaimo since 1921, when prohibition shut down a thriving local brewery scene.

The brewery's best-selling beer is a wheat, which is light amber in color and made with 50% wheat/50% barley malt. It features more of a spicy, hoppy aroma than the usual fruity aroma associated with a wheat. It also makes a Premium lager, which is crisp and full-bodied, using a variety of hops and two-row barley and cara-pils malts and the Rail Ale, a dark amber Pale Ale.

Bastion also brews on contract for two pubs located next door to each other in Nanaimo. Muddy Waters Pub and Millers Landing serve this smooth Cream Ale as Muddy's Draft. The first seasonal beer was a strong, dark brown Christmas Ale with clove and cinnamon flavors coming from a special yeast strain.

Established: 1995

Hours: Tours by appointment

Children: Yes

Food: No

Entertainment: No

Smoking: No

Payment: Checks, Visa/MC

Takeout: Kegs only

Directions: Call for directions.

Bastion Brewing Company

OKANAGAN
VALLEY
BREW
TOUR

The Okanagan Valley has the makings for an excellent brewery tour. Situated in the rainshadow of the Cascades, the Okanagan Valley is dry and sunny most of the year. The region offers several ski slopes, the expansive and picturesque Okanagan Lake, stunning mountain vistas and endless fruit orchards.

Your first stop should rightfully be Buchanan Brewing at Oroville, Washington, the southern gateway to the Okanagan Valley. Operated by Rich Buchanan and Jerry Oakes, both formerly of Redhook, the Buchanan Brewing Company is a cozy pub frequented by both locals and Canadians slipping across the border to buy gas and groceries.

A short drive north through stark brown and orange canyonlands brings the thirsty tourist to the town of Penticton. Located on the southern shores of Okanagan Lake, this is a summer tourist town for folks from Vancouver in search of a beach getaway. The first stop for the brew enthusiast is The Tin Whistle. This is a microbrewery designed for visitors, with taps for tasting right out front and the whole brewhouse, bottling and kegging facility all in the same room. Tours begin with each walk-in group.

Continue north to the town of Kelowna (an indigenous name for the grizzly bear), situated on the northern shores of Okanagan Lake. This is a charming city with delightful waterfront walks. Or, try a short hike at the edge of town, and enjoy a view of the expansive lake. The area's only brewpub, Black Mountain Brewpub & the Schoolhouse Cafe, is situated at the east edge of town. A visit to this eclectic pub can fill a whole evening. Tree Brewing offers day time tours in the industrial section of Kelowna. There are also plans for a second large brewpub.

The next town up the valley is Vernon, home of Okanagan Spring Brewery. "OK Spring," as it's known locally, is one of BC's largest microbreweries. It's housed in a set of unassuming warehouses near Vernon's city center and offers tours (call ahead) and a retail store. The brewery was recently remodeled and expanded and is well worth the stop.

North past Vernon, the valley climbs upward into majestic mountain terrain and the road splits. Both directions leads to a microbrewery – east is Mount Begbie Brewing in Revelstoke, and west is Bear Brewing in Kamloops. Either of these make an exciting conclusion to your brew tour of the Okanagan Valley.

Tin Whistle Brewing Company

954 W. Eckhardt Avenue
Penticton, BC V2A 2C1
604/770-1122

Tin Whistle is a cottage brewery set in an Old West-style building and designed as a tourist attraction. Penticton is a hot spot for summer tourists from the Vancouver area. The entire brewing process is set up in a small space for viewing from the front walk-in area, which doubles as a retail store.

The brewery was named for the first beat-up, old locomotive to run on the Kettle Valley Railroad that serviced the area in the early 20th century. Photos of this old railway adorn the walls of the brewery. This is a true family operation, run by siblings Lawrie Lock and Linda Grierson and their spouses.

The brewhouse was designed by the legendary brewery consultant Frank Appleton (who happens to live in the hills outside of Penticton) and built by Ripley Stainless from neighboring Summerland, BC. The beers are filtered and are distributed throughout the Okanagan Valley, the lower mainland and Vancouver Island.

The brewing company offers three ales, all named for indigenous wildlife and all geared toward the tourist's palate, qualifying as "cross-over" (see Glossary, page 165) beers for the micro novice. Coyote Ale is light, sweet and tasty. Black Widow Dark is a dark ale with plenty of chocolate malts and a fair amount of hops for a Canadian brew. Rounding out the line-up is Rattlesnake Extra Special Bitter.

Established: 1995

Hours: Brewery tours daily. Retail Store: Winter: 11 am-5 pm Monday-Saturday; Summer: 11 am-7 pm Monday-Sunday

Children: Yes

Food: No

Entertainment: No

Smoking: Yes

Payment: Checks, Visa/MC

Takeout: Yes

Directions: Highway 97 becomes Eckhardt Avenue as it enters town. The brewery is at the south end of town, just before the last stoplight, across from the golf course.

Hand Crafted Ales · THE TIN WHISTLE · BREWING COMPANY · Brewed in the Okanagan

Black Mountain Brewpub/Schoolhouse Café
2040 Old Joe Riche Road (RR#5)
Kelowna, BC V1X 4K4
604/491-1020

Established: 1996

Hours: Pub: 10 am-midnight Monday-Sunday. Cafe: 7 am-11 pm Monday-Sunday

Children: Yes, in the cafe

Food: Country cooking-style pub fare

Entertainment: Pool, shuffleboard, library

Smoking: Yes, in separate rooms

Payment: Visa/MC, Am Ex, Interac

Takeout: No

Directions: From Highway 97, turn east on Highway 33. Follow 33 to Springfield Road, located at the end of town. Turn right and drive 1/2 km past Springfield and turn right on Joe Riche Road. The brewpub is on your left.

This multiple environment brewpub is set in an old schoolhouse and is a great stop for summer tourists or folks on the way to Big White Mountain to ski. The first indication of the extent to which the school theme is played up is the sign which offers the greeting "Welcome, report to office."

On the right is the cafe, which is divided into the non-smoking Lunchroom, equipped with tables that resemble old-style school desks, and the smoker-friendly Library, replete with shelves of books. Both seating areas are decorated with children's artwork from the nearby modern schoolhouse.

Black Mountain Brewpub Schoolhouse Café

On the left are the two pub areas. Upstairs is the non-smoking Geography Room, which features pull-down maps of the continents, high tables, a bar and a wall-mounted shuffleboard game. Downstairs is the smokers' pub, the Detention Room with low tables, a bar, pool tables and a jukebox cranking out a mix of tunes loud enough to entertain all pub patrons. No opportunity to exploit the school theme has been missed – chalk boards are everywhere and a game of hopscotch on your way to the restroom is mandatory.

Brewer Mike Nouwen has launched the establishment with a line-up of filtered ales and will soon offer a pair of lagers. The ales include Rodeo Red (lightly-hopped), Big White Brown, Okanagan Honey Ale, which gets the flavor but not the sweetness from the honey, and Black Mountain Black, a porter. The brewhouse is tucked away in the basement along with three open fermenters.

Tree Brewing Company

1083 Richter Street
Kelowna, BC V1Y 2K6
604/860-8836

Tree Brewing is Kelowna's first local microbrewery. The facility is quite large and will soon include a retail store offering Tree Brewing collectibles and Tree's beers in both bottles and kegs. The 20,000-hectoliters (16,800 barrels) annual capacity brewery is comprised of various used equipment, including quite a collection of grundies and European horizontal conditioning tanks.

One of the brewery's most impressive features is a sizable lagering cold room, which is specially insulated and includes a door with a built-in filter. This filter will protect the fermenting beer from the high level of airborne wild yeasts that come from Okanagan Valley's extensive fruit production. President Geoff Twyman is intrigued by the abundance of wild yeasts and is considering an experiment with a Lambic-style beer fermented in the open air of the valley's orchards. Look for Tree Brewing's beers in bottles and on draft throughout the Okanagan Valley. They should begin reaching the lower mainland sometime in the future.

Brewmaster Kendrick Belau is a graduate of the prestigious Braumeister program at the Technical University of Weihenstephan in Munich. He's launching Tree's line of filtered beers with an ale and a lager. The ale is a full-bodied Northwest-style Amber Ale which, according to sales/distribution manager Dave Willoughby, will be a bolder, more complex brew than most of the beers in the Okanagan area. The lager is European, which Belau describes as crisper and more flavorful than most Canadian lagers. The first planned seasonal will be a Christmas Ale.

Established: 1996

Hours: Retail Store: 9 am-5 pm Monday-Saturday, Brewery: Tours on the hour

Children: Yes

Food: No

Entertainment: No

Smoking: No

Payment: Checks, Visa/MC

Takeout: Yes

Directions: From Highway 97, after crossing the bridge over the lake into the heart of town, turn west on Richter Street. Follow Richter about 15 blocks to the large building on the right containing Granville Island Brewing, Calona Wines and, further down the street, Tree Brewing.

Okanagan Spring Brewery

2801 27th Avenue
Vernon, BC V1T 1T5
604/542-2337

Okanagan Spring was inland BC's first microbrewery. Founded by the Tobler father and son team, the brewery has grown to become BC's largest producer of micros, and the company's stock is now publicly traded.

Son Stefan Tobler was professionally trained at the Ulm Brewing School in Germany. The name Okanagan Spring has ties to the brewery's German heritage as well, namely the German tradition of using the word "spring" as a suffix on a brewery's name. The production facility is split between two buildings with brew lines running between them underground. On the brewery tour, look for the three enormous lager tanks built sideways into a wall.

Okanagan Spring beers are distributed throughout BC and Alberta and will soon be available in California. Their most widely available beers are the Lager, the Pale Ale and the Brown Ale. Their other brews are a Pilsner, St. Patrick's Stout, a traditionally styled Hefeweizen made with 60% wheat and a bottle-fermented Old English Porter.

Established: 1985

Hours: Brewery tours: Thursday and Friday or call to arrange one. Retail store: 10 am-5 pm Monday-Friday

Children: Yes

Food: No

Entertainment: No

Smoking: No

Payment: Visa/MC

Takeout: Yes

Directions: From Highway 97, turn east on 28th Avenue and drive three blocks. The brewery is on your right.

Bear Brewing Company
975-B Notre Dame Drive
Kamloops, BC V2C 5P8
604/851-2543

Established: 1995

Hours: Call to arrange a tour

Children: Yes

Food: No

Entertainment: No

Smoking: No

Bear Brewing is a straightforward micro-brewery, with no tasting room or retail store, but tours are provided to interested visitors. Situated in the town of Kamloops, this micro is penetrating the heart of the interior North American commercial beer culture with good, true-to-style craft beers.

Partner/brewer Dave Beardsell holds a degree in microbiology and was formally trained in brewing at Doemen's in Munich and at the Brewing Research Institute in Nutfield, England. After working for Okanagan Spring Brewery (see page 160), he teamed up with Brian Keast to start Bear Brewing.

Beardsell incorporated many tricks he learned in England and Germany into the new venture. The system is all self-designed, including a German- style mash tun and a British-style mash/lauter tun. He imitated Yorkshire stone open-fermentation tanks with concrete tanks that are chilled prior to adding the wort and pitching the yeast. This is quite a departure from the conventional stainless steel fermentation tanks.

Payment: Checks

Takeout: Kegs only

Directions: From Highway 1, take the northern-most City Center exit and turn west on Notre Dame Drive. Follow Notre Dame until it begins to curve uphill. The brewery is on the left.

Draft beers are distributed throughout interior BC and Vancouver. The two standards are Brown Bear Ale, a Northern English-style Brown, full-bodied with lots of chocolate malt; and Polar Bear Lager, a creamy, lagered ale with low carbonation, made with specialty Belgian malts.

Bear also brews the same contract beers for Earl's Restaurant chain in Alberta and Saskatchewan that Bowen Island Brewing (see page 145) brews for Earl's BC locations. These contract recipes are the same – Albino Rhino and four seasonals – but owing to significant differences in brewing methods, the resulting beers tend to be quite different. Also, in the Cherry Stout recipe, Bowen Island uses Bing cherries, whereas Bear uses sour cherries.

Nelson Brewing Company

512 Latimer Street
Nelson, BC V1L 4T9
604/352-3582

Established: 1991

Hours: Call to arrange a tour

Children: Yes

Food: No

Entertainment: No

Smoking: No

Payment: No retail sales

Takeout: No

Eastern BC's first modern microbrewery, Nelson Brewing Company is a reincarnation of the old Nelson Brewing Company, which operated from 1894 until 1955. Owner Paddy Glenny re-established the brewery in late 1990 at the same location and sold his first beer in 1991.

The brewhouse is a 10-barrel system with two 20-barrel open fermenters. The equipment was designed and installed by Glenny himself, who owned a brewery for over a decade in Oxford, England. Glenny also refurbished a 1960s bottling line obtained from a brewery in Eastern Canada, and Nelson Brewing is now sending out bottled and kegged beer to the East and West Kootenays, as well as to the Okanagan Valley and the lower mainland.

Beers include Old Brewery Ale, a true-to-style classic British Pale Ale, lightly hopped for increased quaffability; Nelson Afterdark, a dark English-style Brown Mild; Valhalla Gold, a classic Canadian-style Cream ale; and Nelson Strong Ale, a 6% alcohol/volume India Pale Ale. In 1997, the City of Nelson celebrates its centennial, and Nelson Brewing is in the process of designing a special brew to commemorate the anniversary.

Nestled at the foot of the majestic Kootenay Range, Nelson is a great stop for outdoors enthusiasts enjoying the area's breathtaking scenery. Whether you've been hiking in the Kootenays, mountaineering on the Kokanee Glacier or skiing at Whitewater Hill, Nelson is the stop to make for beer.

Directions: As you pull into Nelson, Highway 3 and Highway 6 become Baker. Turn uphill onto Ward Street and proceed to Latimer Street. The brewery is the large Victorian industrial-style building on the corner of Ward and Latimer. The firehouse across the street is the one used in the film, "Roxanne."

Kimberley Brewing Company, 816 5th Avenue, Kimberley, BC V1A 2T6, 604/427-5320, 888/546-2739

This microbrewery in the "Bavarian City in the Rockies" plans a Bavarian- style lager for its flagship beer, aptly chosen to fit the city's Bavarian cultural and architectural theme. Initial distribution of bottles and kegs will cover both the East and West Kootenays. The brewery will feature a tasting room and a retail store. The store will offer retail sales of both kegs and bottles, as well as Kimberley Brewing collectibles. Regular brewery tours will be offered.

Cog & Kettle Pub & Restaurant, Campbell River, BC

This large brewpub will be upper Vancouver Island's first. Located in the Merecroft Village development, it will feature a full menu with local-style foods as well as more international fare.

Windermere Valley Brewing, Invermere, BC, 604/342-7362

Windermere Valley Brewing will be a small cottage brewery geared for distribution in the East Kootenays draft market. The brewery will make a dry-hopped India Pale Ale and a Blonde ale, and will include a retail store.

Mount Begbie Brewing, Revelstoke, BC, 604/834-2756

Mount Begbie Brewing will soon bring ales to inland BC. The Begbie Cream Ale, Extra Special Bitter and British-style light Brown ale are the first planned brews. Mount Begbie's ales will be available on draft in Revelstoke and surrounding towns, as well as for sale in kegs at the brewery's retail store.

Brewing Terminology Glossary

Additives Chemical products such as enzymes and preservatives used by large-scale breweries to simplify the brewing process, maintain the beer's head and clarify and/or preserve the beer.

Adjunct A supplemental grain, such as rice or corn, used in addition to malted barley, usually by large-scale breweries, to cut brewing costs. Used also as flavor mellowers for astringent barley strains such as six-row.

Ale A top-fermented beer brewed in a traditional style at 50°-68° F for about one week, and exhibiting strong and visible yeast characteristics.

Alpha Acid A sticky resin present in hops which imparts bitterness *(also called* to the finished beer. *humulone)*

Altbier or Alt A traditional German-style ale that is full-bodied with *(literally: old-* pronounced malt flavors and a full hop aroma. *style beer)*

Amber A traditional German-style ale, full-bodied and amber-colored with pronounced malt flavors. Traditional amber beers include Oktoberfest beers, Vienna-style beers and Märzenbiers.

Aroma The initial stage of a taste, yielding first impressions, and often most characterized by hops or yeast.

Auger A pipe-like pump device used to transport grains within the brewery.

Barrel A unit of measure equal to 31 U.S. gallons (bbl) or approximately 124 liters.

Barley The grain of choice for malting and brewing since three or four millennia BCE.

Barley Wine	A traditional British-style beer, high in alcohol content, medium-bodied, very lightly hopped and often sweet.
Beer Engine	A faucet device invented in the 1700s that allows a bartender to pull beer straight from a conditioning cask, resulting in a delicately carbonated glass of beer. (See also Tap.)
Best (Ale)	A traditional British prefix attached to an ale name denoting it as that brewery's proudest offering of that variety (e.g., Best Bitter, Best Brown).
Bitter	A traditional English pub-style ale, with characteristic dry flavors produced by the hops added to the brewing process, full body and a copper or amber color. It has a rich malt taste and a distinct hop bitterness. Variants of bitter ales include Extra Special Bitter, Light Ale, Pale Ale and India Pale Ale.
Bittering Hops	Hops added to the sweet wort early in the boil to bitter it.
Blonde *(also called Golden)*	A descriptor used to refer to a light-colored beer.
Bock	A traditional German-style beer that has a high alcohol content and is richly malted with a hint of sweetness. (See also Doppelbock.)
Body *(also called mouthfeel)*	The quality of the beer that provides the sensation of fullness in the mouth, created by dextrins and proteins.
Boil	Process of cooking the sweet wort with hops to create the wort for fermentation.
Bottle-Conditioned	Carbonated by a secondary fermentation occuring in the bottle.

Bottom-Fermenting Yeast	A type of yeast, used in brewing lagers, that ferments at lower temperatures than top-fermenting yeasts, clumps together (flocculates) relatively late and sinks to the bottom of the fermenter.
Brew	To make beer from malt and other ingredients by means of steeping, boiling and fermentation. The term is also used in the vernacular as a synonym for beer.
Brewhouse	The place in the brewery where the preparation of the wort occurs, consisting primarily of the mash tun, lauter tun and kettle; sometimes including whirlpools, hop jacks, etc. The term has also now entered the vernacular as a synonym for brewpub.
Brewpub	A public drinking establishment that serves beers brewed on premise, often also serving food in a restaurant atmosphere.
Bright Tank	A brewery vessel used for storing a finished beer ready for disbursement into kegs or bottles.
Brown Ale	A traditional-style beer, medium in alcohol content, dark in color, and relatively sweet in flavor with little hops bitterness.
Carbonation	The process of dissolving carbon dioxide gas in a liquid, such as beer.
Cask-Conditioning *(also called real ale)*	A type of ale fermentation wherein a residual sugar foodsource and living yeast are added to the beer as it is barreled, causing secondary fermentation in the barrel. After being given time to settle, the beer is then served on draft, with a very light level of carbonation.
Cellar	The place in the brewery where the fermentation of the beer occurs, along with its storage, bottling and kegging. The fermentation equipment includes conditioning tanks, bright tanks, filters, etc.
Chill Haze	Particulates that form in beer and make it cloudy when chilled.

Clarifier	A substance used to remove or prevent chill haze.
Clarity	The absence of chill haze or particulates in general in a finished beer.
Conversion	The process of malt enzymes changing grain starch into sugar during the mash process.
Cold-condition *(also referred to as lagering the ale)*	A method of finishing an ale's fermentation in which the beer is stored at temperatures usually used for lagers. This tends to lend the finished product a smoother, creamier consistency than standard ales.
Cold-filter	An inexact method of filtration in which the beer is chilled and the yeast is allowed to precipitate out of solution. This is basically a fancy name for conditioning.
Conditioning Tank	A brewery vessel used for completing a beer's aging process after primary fermentation has occurred.
Continental Light	A traditional German- and Dutch-style lager, with characteristic full body, golden color and light hop bitterness and aroma
Continental Dark	A traditional Munich-style beer, with characteristic malt body, brown color and mild hopping, though dryer than a brown ale.
Cottage Brewery	A small microbrewery, commonly one producing 10,000 barrels or less annually.
Craft Brewery	A catch-all term for any size brewery producing fine, hand-crafted beers without adjuncts or pasteurization.
Cream Ale	A traditional American-style beer that is light-bodied and very malty.
Cross-Over Beers	Beers brewed primarily to appeal to novice microbrew drinkers, usually light in body and lightly-hopped.
Decoct	To extract by boiling.

Dextrins	Complex carbohydrates that provide body in beer.
Doppelbock	A traditional German-style beer, high in alcohol content, medium-bodied, very lightly hopped and often sweet. (See also Bock.)
Dry	A descriptor used to characterize beer, in which bitterness dominates over sweetness. (See also Sweet.)
Dry Hopping	The process of adding hops to the wort in the fermenter. Hops are usually added after the boil.
Dunkelweizen	A traditional German-style wheat beer, medium- to heavy-bodied, and medium to dark in color.
Extra Special Bitter *(ESB, also known as a best bitter)*	A traditional variant of a British bitter ale, and the brewery's proudest bitter offering.
Esters	Aromas and flavors, particularly those at the onset and finish of a taste, resulting primarily from yeast.
Fermentation	An enzymatic process occuring in yeast's metabolism, in which an organic molecule of sugar is split into two ethyl alcohol molecules and two carbon dioxide molecules.
Fermenter	A brewery vessel in which the yeast is pitched into the wort and the resulting primary fermentation occurs.
Filter	Any of a variety of devices used to remove yeast and other sediments from a finished beer to achieve clarity and brightness prior to consumption.
Finings	Any substance used to help yeast settle out after fermentation.
Finish	The final stage of a taste, yielding final impressions and often most characterized by hops or yeast.
Finishing Hops	Hops added to the wort late in the boil to impart aroma.

Flocs	The solid particulates of yeast and proteins that clump together and settle out of the beer during fermentation in the process known as flocculation.
Gallon	A U.S. unit of measure equal to 3.79 liters or 128 U.S. fluid ounces.
Golden *(Also called Blonde)*	A descriptor used to refer to a light-colored beer.
Grist	Milled malted grains.
Grundy	A small brewery vessel used as either a fermenter or a storage tank.
Hand-crafted	A tradesman or artisan term referring to the selection of choice ingredients, and the adherence to the goal of not compromising quality in the name of quantity.
Hectoliter	A unit of measure equal to 100 liters or .84 barrels.
Hefeweizen	A traditionally cloudy German-style beer, brewed with wheat instead of (or in addition to) barley, with medium body, creamy malts and a distinctly different yeast flavor.
Hops	An aromatic vine whose female flower cones are dried and used to spice and clarify beer, as well as to preserve it. A member of the morning glory family and a close relative of cannabis. Common hops varieties include such European classics as Northern Brewer (Germany), East Kent Golding (U.K.), Saaz (Czech Republic), Hallertauer Hersbrucker (Germany), Lublin (Poland), Strisslespalt (France) and domestics like Cascade, Centennial, Chinook, Fuggle, Nugget and Willamette.
Hop Jack *(also called a hop back)*	A device used to remove the hops from the wort after the wort has been cooked.

India Pale Ale *(IPA)*	A traditional British, deep-amber variant of a Bitter ale, with a heavier body and stronger hop taste than a standard bitter.
Keg	A unit of measure equal to ½ barrel or 15½ U.S. gallons.
Kettle	A brewery vessel in which the wort is cooked prior to fermentation.
Kilning	The process of heating germinated grains to form malt.
Kölsch	One of only two official names for beer. The name reflects its geographic origin, Cologne, Germany (Köln). It is a golden beer, cold-conditioned but fermented with an ale yeast. (See also Trappist.)
Krausen *(literally: crown)*	The head of foam that forms on the surface of the wort as fermentation reaches its peak.
Lager *(literally: to store)*	A bottom-fermented beer brewed in a traditional style at 41°-50° F for about two weeks for primary fermentation, and 32°-38° F for about four or five weeks for secondary fermentation. It is not a style of beer but rather a method of production. Lager is also used as a verb referring to a method of cold-conditioning an ale to yield a smooth, creamy finished product.
Lambic	A traditional Belgian-style wheat beer, fermented in the open air with fruit and wild yeast and aged for years.
Lauter Tun	A brewery vessel in which the mash is separated from the sweet wort.
Light Ale	A traditional British variant of a bitter ale with lower alcohol content than a standard bitter.
Malt Extracts	Syrup or powder made by evaporating sweet wort and used later for beer making, primarily by home-brewers.

Malt *(also called* *malted barley)*	Barley or other grain which has been soaked, allowed to germinate (sprout), then dried and/or roasted in a heating process called kilning. Sprouting allows the development of enzymes which lead to starch conversion in the mash. This prepares the grain for mashing and the resulting extraction of sweet wort. The sprouting of the grain allows the development of enzymes which lead to starch conversion in the mash. A wide variety of malting processes yield many kinds of malts, including such common examples as pale, six-row, two-row, crystal (caramel), dextrin (carapils), black patent, chocolate, Munich and Vienna.
Märzenbier *(literally:* *March beer)*	A traditional German-style amber ale, brewed in March (which was the end of the brewing season prior to modern cooling systems) for autumn consumption. The most famous is Oktoberfest.
Mash	Process of cooking malted barley in water to extract the complex sugars in preparation for the yeast to ferment. Also used to refer to the spent (or sparged) grains left after the mashing and lautering processes.
Mash Tun	A brewery vessel in which the mashing process occurs.
Microbrewery	A brewery of limited size (commonly less than 20,000 barrels annual production), producing hand-crafted beers. The term is used in the vernacular as a synonym for Craft Brewery.
Mill	The device used for cracking the malted grains in preparation for mashing.
Noble Hops	Hops of relatively low alpha acid content but with superior aromatic and flavor potential, used for both bittering and finishing.
Nutbrown	A traditional British-style beer, medium in alcohol content, dark in color and relatively sweet in flavor with a pronounced nutty flavor and aroma.
Oktoberfest *(literally:* *October* *festival beer)*	A traditional German-style amber ale (see Märzenbier), brewed in the spring for consumption in the fall, and consumed at traditional festivals.

Original Gravity *(also known as starting gravity)*	The specific gravity of the wort prior to fermentation. (See also Terminal Gravity.)
Pale Ale	A traditional British variant of Bitter Ale, with a higher alcohol content, more hops flavor and often darker color than a standard bitter.
Pasteurization	A heating process that kills micro-organisms such as bacteria in beer and other liquids.
Pilsner	A traditional Czech-style lager, with characteristic light yet distinct body, light color and full hop aroma and flavor.
Pitch	To add yeast to wort to begin the fermentation process.
Porter	A traditional British-style ale, light- to medium-bodied, lightly hopped and dark brown to black in color, but lacking a Stout's burnt flavors.
Primary Fermentation	The initial stage of fermentation, characterized by very active yeast conversion of the wort's sugars into alcohol and carbon dioxide. (See also Secondary Fermentation.)
Rack	To transfer beer from one vessel to another, leaving sediment behind.
Rauch Bier *(literally: smoke beer)*	A traditional German-style beer utilizing malted barley roasted over beechwood to give the beer a distinct flavor of smoke.
Red Ale	A traditional Irish-style ale, medium-bodied, lightly or heavily hopped and reddish or copper in color.
Reinheitsgebot	A 1516 Bavarian law, in effect throughout Germany until the advent of the World Trade Organization in the late 1980s, stating that only malted barley, hops, water and yeast (added upon its discovery in the late 19th century) be used to make beer. A lesser-known cousin of the law is still in effect in Norway.

Rogenbier *(literally: rye beer)*	A traditional German style of beer brewed with at least some rye malt.
Running Ale	An ale brewed to be consumed immediately. (See also Stock Ale.)
Rye	A grain sometimes used in beer making, in a secondary role to barley.
Scotch Ale	A traditional Scottish style of beer that is high in alcohol content, medium-bodied and lightly to heavily hopped, with complex malts.
Scottish Ale	A traditional Scottish-style beer, similar to Scotch Ale, but lower in alcohol content and lighter bodied.
Secondary Fermentation	The latter stage of fermentation, characterized by slow yeast conversion of the wort's sugars into alcohol and carbon dioxide. (See also Primary Fermentation.)
Session Ale	A traditional English-style beer, medium-bodied, lightly hopped and moderate in alcohol content, and therefore ideal for drinking during business meetings/meals.
Sparge	To rinse the mashed grains with water in order to extract all the sugars into the resulting sweet wort.
Specialty Malt	Malt which develops a strong flavor, dark color or other specific qualities due to the method of preparation.
Specific Gravity	A measure of liquid density expressed in Specific Gravity Points, and used to predict the alcohol content of the finished brew.
Stock Ale	An ale brewed to age (to hold in stock or inventory). (See also Running Ale.)
Stout	A traditional British-style ale, extremely full-bodied, lightly or heavily hopped and very dark in color with a distinct burnt flavor and aroma. Traditional styles include the Imperial Stout (hoppier) and the Cream Stout (smoother).

Strong Ale	A traditional British-style beer, high in alcohol content, medium-bodied, very lightly hopped and often sweet. Traditional styles of strong ale include Dark, Old, Stock and Barley Wines.
Sweet	A descriptor used to describe beer, etc., in which sweetness dominates over bitterness. (See also Dry.)
Sweet Wort *(also called sweet liquor)*	The liquid created during the mashing process, consisting of malted-barley sugars and enzymes suspended in water.
Tap	A faucet device that utilizes carbon dioxide to push beer from a keg, resulting in a fully carbonated glass of beer. (See also Beer Engine.)
Terminal Gravity *(also known as present gravity and final gravity)*	The specific gravity of the beer after fermentation. (See also Specific Gravity.)
Top-Fermenting Yeast	A yeast used in brewing ales, that ferments at higher temperatures than bottom-fermenting yeasts, clumps together relatively early in the fermentation and is carried up into the kraeusen by carbon dioxide bubbles.
Trappist Ale	One of only two official names for beer, this traditional Belgian-style beer was developed by monks. It is high in alcohol content, medium-bodied, very lightly hopped and often sweet with a distinct flavor derived from strains of yeast. (See also Kölsch.)
Trub	Settled particulates from the boiling and fermentation processes. Types include "hot break trub," hop particles and coagulated protein left in kettle after the boil; and "cold break trub," colloidal protein and dead yeast cells that settle in the fermentation tank.
Vienna	A traditional Austrian-style amber ale, full-bodied and amber-colored with pronounced malt flavors.

Wee Heavy	A traditional Scottish-style ale, very full-bodied, but low in alcohol content.
Weissbier *(literally: wheat beer)*	A traditional German-style wheat beer brewed with at least some wheat malt.
Weizen *(literally: wheaten)*	A traditionally clear German-style beer, brewed with wheat instead of barley, with medium body, light malts and a distinct yeast flavor.
Wheat	A grain sometimes used in beer making, in a secondary role to barley.
Whirlpool	A device used to remove the hops, protein and other sediment from the wort after the boil.
Wit *(literally: white)*	A traditional Belgian-style ale, very light in color and body, very lightly hopped and often sweet.
Wort	The liquid created by boiling the sweet wort with hops and any clarifying agents in preparation for fermentation; the primary ingredient of the finished brew.
Yeast	Relatively large micro-organisms that cause fermentation by consuming sugars and releasing alcohol and carbon dioxide as byproducts. Common brewing strains include ale yeasts such as German, Scottish Ale, British, American Ale, Bavarian Wheat and Belgian Abbey, and lager yeasts such as Pilsen, Danish, Californian, Bohemian and Munich.
Zymurgy	The study of yeast.

You-Brew/Brew-On-Premise Facilities
(Alphabetical by Place)

British Columbia

Burnaby Brewing Company Ltd.
2-3051 Underhill
Burnaby, BC
604/421-2929 or 421-2911

Hillcrest Brewing Company Ltd.
1-7541 Conway
Burnaby, BC
604/432-7727

BA Brewmaster Ltd.
20-1425 Cariboo Place
Kamloops, BC
604/372-2739

Brewland, Inc.
455 Lansdowne
Kamloops, BC
604/372-1332

High Country Brewing House
2-2101 E. Trans-Canada Highway
Kamloops, BC
604/374-5757

Aunt Maryann's U-Brewtique
1A-1368 Street Paul
Kelowna, BC
604/861-5161

Brew Tech Ltd.
1809 Baron
Kelowna, BC
604/860-4441

Kelowna Brew Club
1B-1415 Hunter Court
Kelowna, BC
604/862-8862

Michael's Beer Factory
180-2000 Spall
Kelowna, BC
604/762-2337

Okanagan Brewhouse, Inc.
I-2250 Leckie Road
Kelowna, BC
604/868-8202

Westside U-Brew
1789 Ross
Kelowna, BC
604/769-6625

Drew's Brews
1960 Quilchena
Merritt, BC
604/378-2832

Powell River Brewing Company
7030 Glacier Street
Powell River, BC V8A 5A1
604/485-0022

Richmond Beer Works
115-7011 Elmbridge Way
Richmond, BC
604/244-8103

Steveston Brewing
Unit 1, 11151 Horseshoe Way
Richmond, BC
604/241-1968

Bayou Brewing Club
12751 Bathgate Way
Richmond, BC
604/270-9965

Bentley's Brewhouse
Richmond, BC
604/276-2337

Avalon Cottage Winery & Brewing Supplies
3-6782 Veyaness
Saanichton, BC
604/652-8818

**Murray's Brew Place/
The Cap & Cork**
121 McPhillips
Salt Spring Island, BC
604/537-1429

Peninsula U-Brew
201-2031 Malaview
Sidney, BC
604/655-7121

Sooke U-Brew
2044 Otter Point Road
Sooke, BC
604/642-7787

Broadway Brewing Company
2860 W. Broadway
Vancouver, BC
604/736-4801

Broadway Brewing Company
5641 Dunbar Street
Vancouver, BC
604/264-9463

Broadway Brewing Company
122 W. Broadway
Vancouver, BC
604/874-2324

Easy Brews
809 Carnarvon NW
Vancouver, BC
604/524-0140

Kitsilano Brewing Company Ltd.
2034 W. 11th
Vancouver, BC
604/731-1108

Marpole Brewmasters Ltd.
750 SW Marine Drive
Vancouver, BC
604/324-2739

Vancouver Brewmasters
3150 W. Broadway
Vancouver, BC
604/734-2739

Westminster Brewing Company
1325 Derwent Way NW
Vancouver, BC
604/521-2337

**Woodhouse Personal Brewery &
Winery**
119-2828 E. Hastings
Vancouver, BC
604/254-4458

Avalon Cottage Winery & Brewing
1157A Newport
Victora, BC
604/595-7770

Brew Byou
871 Station
Victoria, BC
604/474-2550

The Brew Works
4-4144 Wilkinson Road
Victoria, BC
604/744-2739

Fermenthaus
3200 Quadra
Victoria, BC
604/386-1023

Goldstream U-Brew
927 Goldstream
Victoria, BC
604/474-2337

Hamilton Hops & Grapes
464A Burnside E.
Victoria, BC
604/388-4511

West Coast U-Brew
155 Langford Street
Victoria, BC
604/384-8484

Oregon

Brewmasters
375 2nd Street
Bandon, OR
541/347-1195

Brew Your Own Beer
3400 State Street, G710
Salem, OR
503/585-2739

Glisan Street Brewhouse
1402 NW Glisan Street
Portland, OR
503/22-9566

Washington

Chuckanut Bay Brewing
709 W. Orchard Drive
Bellingham, WA
360/734-4223

Gallaghers' Where You Brew
120 5th Avenue S.
Edmonds, WA
206/776-4209

U-Brew Seattle
8515 Greenwood Avenue N.
Seattle, WA
206/782-2537

Brew Masters
6122 Motor SW
Tacoma, WA
206/589-2739

Homebrewing Suppliers

(Alphabetical by Place)

British Columbia

**Spagnol's Winemaking
& Brewing Supplies**
1325 Derwent Way
Annacis Island, BC
604/524-9463

**Hastings Brewers
& Vintners Supply Ltd.**
4347 Hastings
Burnaby, BC
604/294-2551

Brew King
1622 Kebet Way
Coquitlam, BC
604/464-1882

**Okanagan Juice
& Wine Laboratory**
1083 Richter Street
Kelowna, BC
604/860-8836

Wine Art & Other Delights
3-2925 Pandosy
Kelowna, BC
604/763-8479

Sailor Hagar's
235 W. 1st Avenue
North Vancouver, BC
604/984-3087

**Avalon Cottage Winery
& Brewing Supplies**
3-6782 Veyaness
Saanichton, BC
604/652-8818

Peninsula U-Brew
201-2031 Malaview
Sidney, BC
604/655-7121

Pebble Hill Industries, Inc.
208 54th Street
Tsawwassen, BC
604/943-3034

Albi Store
5496 Victoria Drive
Vancouver, BC
604/327-4716

Custom Brew Beer Systems
3492 W. 13th Avenue
Vancouver, BC
604/736-8280

U-Brew Shoppe
1433 Commercial Drive
Vancouver, BC
604/251-3411

Hobby Beers & Wines
1302 Finlayson Street
Victoria, BC
604/382-2739

West Coast U-Brew, Inc.
29 E. 2nd
Vancouver, BC
604/875-0600

The Other Beer Store
4468A W. Saanich
Victoria, BC
604/744-1685

Brew-At-Home
Victoria, BC
604/361-8040

West Coast Brew-Shop
155 Langford Street
Victoria BC
604/384-8484

Oregon

Glorybee Foods
120 N. Seneca Road
Eugene, OR
541/689-0913

Willamette Street Homebrew
1683 Willamette Street
Eugene, OR
541/683-4064

The Home Fermenter Center
123 Monroe Street
Eugene, OR
541/485-6238

F. H. Steinbart
234 SE 12th Avenue
Portland, OR
503/232-8793

Premier Mini-Brewery Kit
3355 N. Delta #193
Eugene, OR
541/729-5078
800/772-6447

Springfield Smoke Shop
1124 Main Street
Springfield, OR
541/747-8529

Ruby Brew
1792 Augusta
Eugene, OR
541/686-9442

Northwest Brewers' Supply
915 Sixth Street
Anacortes, WA
800/460-7095

Evergreen Brewing Supply
12121 NE Northup Way, Ste. 210
Bellevue, WA
206/882-9929
800/789-2739

Chuckanut Bay Brewing
709 W. Orchard Drive
Bellingham, WA
360/734-4223

The Hop Shoppe
7526 Olympic View Drive
Edmonds, WA
206/776-2237

The Homebrewery
3813 Rucker Avenue
Everett, WA
800/850-2739

The Homebrewer's Store
P. O. Box 82736
Kenmore, WA
206/982-5186

**Larry's Warehouse
Brewing Supply**
7405 S. 212th
Kent, WA
206/872-6846

Beer & Wine Craft
371 Lynden-Birch Bay Road
Lynden, WA
360/354-3735

Consolidated Beverages
P. O. Box 714
Medina, WA
206/635-9363

Beer & Wine Making Cellar
14411 Greenwood N.
Seattle, WA
206/365-7660
800/342-1871

Brewer's Warehouse
4520 Union Bay Place NE
Seattle, WA
206/527-5047

Liberty Malt Supply Company
Pike Place Market
1419 1st Avenue
Seattle, WA
206/622-1880

Northwest Brewers' Supply
Company
5963 Carson Avenue S. #176
Seattle, WA
206/736-2679

West Seattle Homebrew Supply
Company
4823 California SW
Seattle, WA
206/932-1202

Jim's Five-Cent Home Brew
2619 N. Division Street
Spokane, WA
509/328-4850
800/326-7769

800 # Suppliers

Alternative Beverages
800/365-2739

Jim's Five-Cent Home Brew
800/326-7769

Beverage People
800/544-1867

New York Homebrew
800/966-2739

Brew Brothers
800/390-2739

Northwest Brewers' Supply
800/460-7095

Brewers' Coop
800/451-6348

Pawtucket Homebrewing Supply
800/871-2739

Brewers' Resource
800/887-2739

Pine Island Cheese Mart
800/596-2739

Evergreen Brewing Supply
800/789-2739

Premier Mini-Brewery Kit
800/772-6447

Fun Fermentations
800/950-9463

Williams Brewing
800/759-6025

The Home Brewery
800/850-2739

Index

Admiral Pub, 92

Alki Tavern, The, 92

Anacortes Brewhouse , 112

Attic Alehouse & Eatery, The, 92

Backstage, The, 92

Ballard Firehouse Food &
    Beverage Company, 92

Bandon Brewing Company , 15

Bank Brewing Company , 16

Bastion Brewing Company , 154

Bear Brewing Company , 161

Belltown Pub, The, 92

Bend Brewing Company , 63

Big Horse Brewing Company , 59

Big Time Brewery, 93

Bighorn Brewing Company, 34

Birkebeiner Brewing
    Company, 125

Black Mountain Brewpub/
    Schoolhouse Café, 158

Blue Moon, The, 91

Blue Mountain Brewing, 65

Blue Pine Brewpub, 21

Bohemian Café, The, 92

Boundary Bay Brewery and
    Bistro, 116

Bowen Island Brewing
    Company Ltd., 148

Bridgeport Brewing Company, 42

Buchanan Brewing Company, 129

Buckerfield's Brewery/
    Swan Hotel, 151

Captain City Brewery/
    Front Street Cafe, 110

Cardiff Arms Alehouse, 92

Cascade Microbrewery & Public
    Firehouse, 35

Chuckanut Bay Brewing
    Company, 117

CJ's Brewpub, 75

Cog & Kettle Pub & Restaurant, 163

College Inn Pub, The, 91

Comet Tavern, 92

Cooper's Alehouse, 91

D

Deschutes Brewing Company, 64

Diamond Knot Brewing Company/Cheers, Too, 106

Dubliner, The, 91

Duchess Tavern, 91

E

Eagle Brewing Company/ Riley's Pizza, 107

Ellensburg Brewing Company, 121

Elysian Brewing Company & Public House, 130

Engine House No. 9 Restaurant & Brewery, 81

Eugene City Brewery, 27

F

Fiddler's Inn, 91

Fish Brewing Company, 80

Fort Spokane Brewery, 124

Full Sail – Hood River, 60

Full Sail at River Place, 43

G

Glacier Peak Brewing Company, 105

Golden Valley Brewery Pub & Restaurant, 37

Grant's Brewery Pub, 122

Granville Island Brewing Company, 142

Greenlake Alehouse, The, 91

H

Hair of the Dog Brewing Company, 44

Hale's Ales (Fremont), 94

Hale's Ales (Spokane), 126

Hazel Dell Brewpub, 76

Hilltop Alehouse, 92

Horseshoe Bay Brewing Company, 147

House of Rogues & Headquarters for Int'l Assoc. of Rogues, 18

I

Issaquah Brewing Company, 86

J

J&M Café, 92

K

Kell's Irish Pub, 92

Kelley Creek Brewing Company, 84

Kerryman Pub & Restaurant, The, 91

Kimberly Brewing Company, 163

L

La Conner Brewing, 114

Latona By Green Lake, The, 91

Leavenworth Brewery, The, 127

Lucky Labrador Brewing Company, 45

M

Mac & Jack's, 130

Mad Dog Alehouse, 92

Maritime Pacific Brewing Company, 96

McMenamins Edgefield Brewery, 58

McMenamins Establishments, 68-71

Mount Begbie Brewing, 163

Mt. Angel Brewing Company, 36

Mt. Hood Brewing Company, 61

Multnomah Brewing Company, 46

Murphy's Pub, 91

N

Nelson Brewing Company, 162

Nor'Wester Public House, 47

North Cascades Brewing Company, 131

North Fork Brewpub, 131

North Sound Brewing, 130

Northern Lights Brewing Company, 123

O

Oak Harbor Pub & Brewery, 111

Okanagan Spring Brewery, 160

Old Chicago, 48

Old Market Pub & Brewery, The, 49

Onalaska Brewing Company, 78

Orchard Street Brewery, 118

Oregon Fields Brewing Company, 28

Oregon Trader Brewing Company, 33

Oregon Trail, 32

Osprey Ale Brewpub, 65

P

Pacific Brewing Company Limited, 97

Pacific Inn Pub, 91

Pelican Pub & Brewery, 65

Philadelphia's Steaks & Hoagies, 50

Pike Brewing Company, 98

Portland Brewing Company, 52

Portland Brewing Company/ Flanders Street Brewpub, 51

Powerhouse Restaurant & Brewery, 82

Pyramid Breweries, Inc., 77, 95

R

Red Door Alehouse, 91

Redhook Ale Brewery - The Trolleyman Pub, 99

Redhook Brewery - Forecasters Brewpub, 85

Redmond Brewing Company, 130

Reservoir Tavern, 91

Rock Bottom Brewery, 53

Rogue Ales Bayfront Public House, 17

Rogue Ales Brewery & South Beach Tasting Room, 18

Roslyn Brewing Company, 120

Russell Brewing, 138

S

Sailor Hagar's Brewpub, 146

San Juan Brewing Company-
Front Street Ale House, 113

Saxer Brewing Company, 38

Seattle Brewers, 100

Seattle Brewing Company/
Aviator Ales, 101

Seventh Street Brew House/
Cascade Lakes Brewing
Company, 62

74th Street Alehouse, 91

Shaftebury Brewing, 137

Siletz Brewing Company, 19

Siskiyou Brewing Company, 20

Skagit River Brewing
Company, 115

Snipes Mountain Brewing, 131

Spencer's Restaurant &
Brewhouse, 31

Spinnakers Brewpub, 152

Star Brewing Company, 54

SteamWorks Brewing
Company, 143

Steelhead Brewing Company, 29

Storm Brewing Company, 144

T

Tall Ship Ale Company
Limited, 149

Tapps Brewing, 83

Teddy's Tavern, 91

Thomas Kemper Brewery, 108

Timberland Brewing Company, 65

Tin Whistle Brewing
Company, 157

Tree Brewing Company, 159

Tugboat Brewing Company, 55

Twin Rivers Brewing Company/
Sailfish Bar & Grill, 87

U

Umpqua Brewing Company, 23

V

Vancouver Island Brewing
Company, 153

Virginia Inn Tavern, The, 92

W

Wedgwood Alehouse & Café, 91

West Seattle Brewing Company/
California & Alaska Street
Brewery, 102

Westside Alehouse, 92

Whatcom Brewery, 119

Whidbey Island Brewing, 130

Whidbey Island Brewing
Company, 109

Whistler Brewing Company, 150

Widmer Brewing & Gasthaus, 57

Widmer Brewing Company, 56

Wild Duck Brewery, the, 30

Wild River Brewing & Pizza
Company, 22

Windermere Valley Brewing, 163

Winthrop Brewing Company, 128

Woodland Park Pub, 91

Y

Yaletown Brewing Company, 145

Youngs Brewing Company, 79

About the Authors

Hudson Dodd lives in Bellingham, Washington with his wife, Mary Kurlinski, and their cat Jester. Hudson works at Western Washington University, is an avid homebrewer, and is always searching for the perfect porter.

Matthew Latterell works as a computer support specialist at the University of Oregon and is Managing Editor of the Willamette Green Directory. A tremendous fan of Northwest hops, Matthew believes that "bitter is always better."

Lani MacCormack is an Account Executive and Media Planner for Cawood Communications, an advertising and public relations firm in Eugene, Oregon. Lani favors ambers and eagerly awaits the opening of Oktoberfest season each year.

Ina Zucker spends most of her time at the LocoMotive, an upscale vegetarian restaurant she and her family recently opened in Eugene, Oregon. She also serves as Editorial Director for the Willamette Green Directory, yet still finds time to enjoy the eclectic flavors of regional red ales.